# THE HAZARDOUS EARTH

# TSUNAMIS

## Giant Waves from the Sea

# TSUNAMIS

## Giant Waves from the Sea

## Timothy Kusky, Ph.D.

Facts On File
An imprint of Infobase Publishing

**TSUNAMIS: Giant Waves from the Sea**

Facts On File, Inc.
An imprint of Infobase Publishing
132 West 31st Street
New York NY 10001

**Library of Congress Cataloging-in-Publication Data**

Kusky, Timothy M.
  Tsunamis : giant waves from the sea / Timothy Kusky.
    p. cm. — (The hazardous Earth)
  Includes bibliographical references and index.
  ISBN-13: 978-0-8160-6464-9
  ISBN-10: 0-8160-6464-4
  1. Tsunamis—Juvenile literature. I. Title.

  GC221.5.K87 2008
  551.46'37—dc22    2007023477

Facts On File books are available at special discounts when purchased in bulk quantities for businesses, associations, institutions, or sales promotions. Please call our Special Sales Department in New York at (212) 967-8800 or (800) 322-8755.

You can find Facts On File on the World Wide Web at
http://www.factsonfile.com

Text design by Erika K. Arroyo
Illustrations by Melissa Ericksen
Photo research by Suzanne M. Tibor

Printed in the United States of America

VB ML 10 9 8 7 6 5 4 3 2 1

This book is printed on acid-free paper and contains 30 percent post-consumer recycled content.

*To those who perished in the December 26, 2004,*
*Indian Ocean tsunami*

■　■　■

# Contents

# Preface

Natural geologic hazards arise from the interaction between humans and the Earth's natural processes. Recent natural disasters such as the 2004 Indian Ocean tsunami that killed more than a quarter million people and earthquakes in Iran, Turkey, and Japan have shown how the motion of the Earth's tectonic plates can suddenly make apparently safe environments dangerous or even deadly. The slow sinking of the land surface along many seashores has made many of the world's coastal regions prone to damage by ocean storms, as shown disastrously by Hurricane Katrina in 2005. Other natural Earth hazards arise gradually, such as the migration of poisonous radon gas into people's homes. Knowledge of the Earth's natural hazards can lead one to live a safer life, providing guidance on where to build homes, where to travel, and what to do during natural hazard emergencies.

The eight-volume The Hazardous Earth set is intended to provide middle- and high-school students and college students with a readable yet comprehensive account of natural geologic hazards—the geologic processes that create conditions hazardous to humans—and what can be done to minimize their effects. Titles in the set present clear descriptions of plate tectonics and associated hazards, including earthquakes, volcanic eruptions, landslides, and soil and mineral hazards, as well as hazards resulting from the interaction of the ocean, atmosphere, and land, such as tsunamis, hurricanes, floods, and drought. After providing the reader with an in-depth knowledge of naturally hazardous processes, each volume gives vivid accounts of historic disasters and events that have shaped human history and serve as reminders for future generations.

One volume covers the basic principles of plate tectonics and earthquake hazards, and another volume covers hazards associated with volcanoes. A third volume is about tsunamis and related wave phenomena, and another volume covers landslides, soil, and mineral hazards, and includes discussions of mass wasting processes, soils, and the dangers of the natural concentration of hazardous elements such as radon. A fifth volume covers hazards resulting from climate change and drought, and how they affect human populations. That volume also discusses glacial environments and landforms, shifting climates, and desertification—all related to the planet's oscillations from ice ages to hothouses. Greater understanding is achieved by discussing environments on Earth that resemble icehouse (glaciers) and hothouse (desert) conditions. A sixth volume, entitled *The Coast*, includes discussion of hazards associated with hurricanes, coastal subsidence, and the impact of building along coastlines. A seventh volume, *Floods*, discusses river flooding and flood disasters, as well as many of the contemporary issues associated with the world's diminishing freshwater supply in the face of a growing population. This book also includes a chapter on sinkholes and phenomena related to water overuse. An eighth volume, *Asteroids and Meteorites*, presents information on impacts that have affected the Earth, their effects, and the chances that another impact may occur soon on Earth.

The Hazardous Earth set is intended overall to be a reference book set for middle school, high school, and undergraduate college students, teachers and professors, scientists, librarians, journalists, and anyone who may be looking for information about Earth processes that may be hazardous to humans. The set is well illustrated with photographs and other illustrations, including line art, graphs, and tables. Each volume stands alone and can also be used in sequence with other volumes of the set in a natural hazards or disasters curriculum.

# Acknowledgments

Many people have helped me with different aspects of preparing this volume. I would especially like to thank Carolyn, my wife, and my children, Shoshana and Daniel, for their patience during the long hours spent at my desk preparing this book. Without their understanding this work would not have been possible. Frank Darmstadt, Executive Editor, reviewed and edited all text and figures, providing guidance and consistency throughout. The excellent photo research provided by Suzie Tibor is appreciated, and she is responsible for locating many of the excellent photographs in this volume. Many sections of the work draw from my own experiences doing scientific research in different parts of the world, and it is not possible to thank the hundreds of colleagues whose collaborations and work I have related in this book.

For this volume I especially thank my colleagues Drs. Li Sanzhong, Wang Lu, and Li Guangxi at the Ocean University of China, who have helped me appreciate land-sea interactions such as tsunamis. Their contributions to the science that allowed the writing of this volume are greatly appreciated. I have tried to reference the most relevant works or, in some cases, more recent sources with extensive reference lists. Any omissions are unintentional.

# Introduction

Every few years, giant waves rise unexpectedly out of the ocean and sweep over coastal communities, killing hundreds or thousands of people and causing millions of dollars in damage. Such events occurred in 1946, 1960, 1964, 1992, 1993, and 1998 in coastal Pacific regions, and in 2004 in the Indian Ocean. In 1998, a catastrophic 50-foot- (15-m-) high wave unexpectedly struck Papua New Guinea, killing more than 2,000 people and leaving more than 10,000 homeless. The 2004 Indian Ocean *tsunami* is estimated to have killed 283,000 people worldwide. What are these giant waves, and what causes them to strike without warning? Tsunamis are seismic sea waves, most of which are generated by the sudden displacement of the seafloor. The most common causes of this sudden displacement are *earthquakes,* landslides, and volcanic eruptions. The name is of Japanese origin, meaning "harbor wave." Tsunamis are also called tidal waves, although this is improper because they have nothing to do with tides.

The following chapters discuss many aspects of the generation, movement, and effects of tsunamis. Chapter 1 discusses the triggering mechanisms for tsunamis, including earthquakes, volcanic eruptions, landslides, and other rarer events. Chapter 2 is dedicated to discussion of the movement of tsunamis, from their fast travel across deep water to their encounters with shallow water and eventual disastrous run-ups into coastal areas. Chapter 3 is about processes similar to tsunamis, including the formation of other types of large waves in enclosed water bodies, storm surges, and tides. Chapter 4 consists of descriptions of

Tourists run from approaching tsunami wave, as a wall of water in the distance approaches a beach in Thailand. The people in this image ran, and survived. *(AFP/Getty Images)*

historical tsunamis, and tsunamis generated by earthquakes, volcanic eruptions, and landslides are all discussed. Chapter 5 is dedicated to analysis and discussion of the greatest tsunami of recorded history, the 2004 Indian Ocean tsunami. In chapter 6, the understanding of the physics and historical effects of tsunamis are put together to discuss the different types of tsunami warning systems and to provide a basis for educating the public in coastal areas about what they need to know about tsunamis in order to be better protected from this threat.

Most tsunamis are generated by *thrust* earthquakes along deep-ocean trenches and *convergent boundaries.* Therefore, tsunamis occur most frequently along the margins of the Pacific Ocean, a region characterized by numerous thrust-type earthquakes. About 80 percent of all tsunamis strike shorelines around the Pacific Ocean, the most generated in and striking southern Alaska. Volcanic eruptions, giant submarine landslides, and the sudden release of gases from sediments on the seafloor may also generate tsunamis. They are not rare on Pacific islands including Hawaii and Japan, which now have extensive warning systems in place to alert residents.

One of the worst natural disasters in history unfolded on December 26, 2004, following a magnitude 9.0 earthquake off the coast of northern Sumatra in the Indian Ocean. This earthquake was the largest since the 1964 magnitude 9.2 event in southern Alaska and released more energy

People flee as the tsunami hits a beach resort in Thailand. *(John Russell/AFP/Getty Images)*

than all the earthquakes on the planet in the last 25 years combined. During this catastrophic earthquake, a segment of the seafloor the size of the state of California, lying above the Sumatra *subduction* zone trench, suddenly moved upward and seaward by more than 30 feet (9 m). The sudden displacement of this volume of undersea floor displaced a huge amount of water and generated the most destructive tsunami known in recorded history.

Within minutes of the initial earthquake, a mountain of water more than 100 feet (30 m) high was ravaging northern Sumatra, sweeping into coastal villages and resort communities with a fury that crushed all in its path, removing buildings, vegetation, and in many cases eroding shoreline areas down to bedrock, leaving no traces of the previous inhabitants or structures. Similar scenes of destruction and devastation spread rapidly throughout Indonesia, where residents and tourists were enjoying a holiday weekend. Firsthand accounts and numerous videos made of the catastrophe reveal similar scenes of horror, where unsuspecting tourists and residents are enjoying themselves in beachfront playgrounds, resorts, and villages and react as large breaking waves appear off the coast. Many moved toward the shore to watch the high surf with interest, then ran in panic as the sea rapidly rose beyond expectations and walls of water engulfed entire beachfronts, rising above hotel lobbies and washing through towns with the force of Niagara Falls. In some cases, the sea retreated to unprecedented low levels before the waves struck, causing many people to move to the shore to investigate the phenomenon. In other cases, the sea waves simply came crashing inland without warning. Buildings, vehicles, trees, boats, and other debris were washed along with the ocean waters, forming projectiles that smashed at speeds of up to 30 MPH (50 km/hr) into other structures, leveling all in their paths, and killing more than one-quarter million people.

The displaced water formed a deepwater tsunami that moved at speeds of 500 MPH (805 km/hr) across the Indian Ocean, smashing within an hour into Sri Lanka and southern India, wiping away entire fishing communities and causing widespread destruction of the shore environment. Ancient Indian legends speak of villages that have disappeared into the sea, stories that many locals now understand as relating times of previous tsunamis, long since forgotten by modern residents. South of India are many small islands including the Maldives, Chagos, and Seychelles, many of which have maximum elevations of only a few to a few tens of feet above normal sea level. As the tsunami approached these islands, wildlife and native tribes fled to the deep forest, sensing the danger as the sea retreated and the ground trembled with the approaching wall of water. As the tsunami was higher than many of the maximum elevations of some of these islands, the forest was able to protect and save many lives in places by causing the sea levels to rise with less force than in places where the shoreline geometry caused large breaking waves to crash ashore.

Several hours later, the tsunami reached the shores of Africa and Madagascar, and, though its height was diminished to under 10 feet (3 m) with distance from the source, several hundred people were killed by the waves and high water. Kenya and Somalia were hit severely, with harbors experiencing rapid and unpredictable rises and falls in sea level and many boats and people washed to sea. Villages in coastal eastern Madagascar, recently devastated by tropical cyclones, were hit by large waves, washing homes and people into the sea and forming new coastal shoreline patterns.

The tsunami traveled around the world with progressively decreasing height, as measured by satellites and ocean bottom pressure sensors more than 24 hours later in the North Atlantic and Pacific Oceans. Overall, more than 283,000 people perished in the December 26 Indian Ocean tsunami. Many might have been saved if a tsunami warning system had been in place. Tsunami warning systems have been developed that are capable of saving many lives by alerting residents of coastal areas that a tsunami is approaching. These systems are most effective for areas located more than 500 miles (805 km), or one hour, away from the source of the tsunami, but may be effective at saving lives in closer areas. The tsunami warning system operating in the Pacific Ocean basin integrates data from several different sources and involves several different government agencies. The National Oceanic and Atmospheric Administration (NOAA) operates the Pacific Tsunami Warning Center in Honolulu. It includes many seismic stations that record earthquakes and quickly sort out those earthquakes that are likely to be tsunamogenic (causing tsunamis) based on their characteristics. A series of tidal gauges placed around the Pacific monitor the passage of any tsunami, and, if they detect a tsunami, warnings are quickly issued for local and regional areas likely to be affected. Analyzing all of this information takes time, however, so this system is most effective for areas located far from the earthquake source.

Tsunami warning systems designed for shorter-term, more local warnings are also in place in many communities, including Japan, Alaska, Hawaii, and many other Pacific islands. These warnings are based mainly on quickly estimating the magnitude of nearby earthquakes and the ability of public authorities to rapidly issue warnings so the population has time to respond. For local earthquakes, the time between the shock event and the tsunami hitting the shoreline may be only a

Two IKONOS satellite images showing the coastal community of Banda Aceh, Indonesia, before (left) and after (right) the tsunami. Towns were completely destroyed and most trees, vegetation, shrimp farms, and buildings were washed away when the tsunami hit with a height at the shore of more than 50 feet (15m). Agricultural lands behind were covered with salt water for days after the tsunami, and sand from the beachfront was completely removed. *(CORBIS)*

few minutes. Anybody in a coastal area who feels a strong earthquake should take that as a natural warning that a tsunami may be imminent and leave low-lying coastal areas. This is especially important considering that approximately 99 percent of all tsunami-related fatalities have historically occurred within 150 miles (250 km) of the tsunami's origin or within 30 minutes of when the tsunami was generated.

The magnitude 9.0 Sumatra earthquake that caused the Indian Ocean tsunami was detected by American scientists who tried to warn countries in soon-to-be-affected regions that a tsunami might be approaching. However, despite previous efforts by some scientists, no systematic warning system was in place in the Indian Ocean. Initial cost estimates for a crude system were about $20 million, deemed too expensive by poor nations who needed the funds for more obviously pressing humanitarian causes. When the earthquake struck on a Sunday, scientists who tried calling and e-mailing countries and communities surrounding the Indian Ocean to warn them of the impending disaster typically found no one in the office and no systematic list of phone numbers of emergency response personnel. Having a simple phone pyramid list could have potentially saved tens of thousands of lives. Indian Ocean communities are now establishing a regional tsunami warning system.

The areas in the United States at greatest risk for large tsunamis border the Pacific, including Hawaii, Alaska, Washington State, Oregon, and California. Most of the future tsunamis in these regions will be generated in subduction zones in Alaska, along the western and southwestern Pacific, and, most frighteningly, along the Cascadia subduction zone in Northern California, Oregon, and Washington. This region has experienced catastrophic tsunamis in the past, with geologists recently recognizing a huge wave that devastated the coast about 300 years ago. The reasons this area presently has the greatest risk in the United States for the largest loss of life and destruction in a tsunami are that it is heavily populated (unlike Alaska) and its coastal areas lie very close to a potentially tsunami-generating subduction zone. Tsunamis travel faster than regular wind-generated waves, at close to 500 MPH (800 km/hr). If the Cascadia subduction zone were to generate a tsunami, coastal areas in this region would have very little time to respond. If distant subduction zones generated a tsunami, the Pacific tsunami warning system could effectively warn coastal areas hours in advance of any crashing waves. However, a large earthquake in the Cascadia subduction zone would immediately wreak havoc on the land by passage of the seismic waves, then minutes to an hour later, potentially send huge waves into coastal Washington, Oregon, and California. There would be little time to react. It is these regions that need to invest most in more sophisticated warning systems, with coastal defenses, warning sirens, publicized and posted evacuation plans, and education of the public about how to behave (run and stay on high ground) in a tsunami emergency. Other coastal areas should initiate ocean-basin-wide warning systems, install warning sirens, and post information on tsunami warnings and evacuation plans. Finally, the general public should be better educated about how to recognize and react to tsunamis and other natural geologic hazards.

What are the lessons to be learned from the tragic Indian Ocean tsunami? People who are near the sea or in an area prone to tsunamis (as indicated by warning signs in places like Hawaii) need to pay particular attention to some of the subtle and not so subtle warning signs that a tsunami may be imminent. First, there may be warning sirens in an area that is equipped with a tsunami warning system. If the sirens sound an alert, do not waste time. Run to high ground immediately. People in more remote locations may need to pay attention to natural warning signs. Anyone who feels an earthquake while on the coast should run for higher ground. There may only be minutes before a tsunami hits, maybe an hour or two or never, but it is better to be safe than sorry. It is important to remember that tsunamis travel in groups, with periods between crests that can be an hour or more. So do not go back to the beach to investigate the damage after the first crest passes. If the tsunami-generating earthquake occurred far away and there is no *ground motion* in the area, there may not be any warning of the impending tsunami, except for the thunderous crash of waves as it rises into the coastal area. In other cases, the water may suddenly recede to unprecedented levels right before it quickly rises up again in the tsunami crest. In either case, anyone enjoying the beach needs to remain aware of the dangers. Campers should pick a sheltered spot where the waves might be refracted and not run up so far. In general, the heads of bays receive the highest run-ups and the sides and mouths record lower run-up heights. This may vary considerably, depending on the submarine topography and other factors.

Other tsunamis have been absolutely devastating to coastal communities, wiping out entire populations with little warning. One of the most devastating tsunamis in recent history was generated by the eruption of the Indonesian volcano Krakatau in 1883. When Krakatau erupted, it blasted a large part of the center of the volcano out, and seawater rushed in to fill the hole. This seawater was immediately heated, and it exploded outward in a steam eruption and a huge wave of hot water. The tsunami generated by this eruption reached more than 120 feet (36 m) in height and killed more than 36,500 people in nearby coastal regions. Another famous tsunami was also generated by the volcanic eruption of Santorini (now called Thera) in the Aegean Sea. In 1650 B.C.E., this volcano was the site of the most powerful eruption in recorded history, and it generated a tsunami that destroyed many Mediterranean coastal areas and probably led to the downfall of the Minoan civilization on Crete. The tsunami deposited volcanic debris at elevations of up to 800 feet (244 m) above the mean ocean level on the nearby island of Anaphi and was still more than 20 feet (6 m) high when it ran up the shorelines on the far side of the Mediterranean in Israel.

# 1

# Triggering Mechanisms for Tsunamis

This chapter examines the origin of the giant sea waves known as tsunamis. Tsunamis may be generated by any event that suddenly displaces the seafloor, which in turn causes the seawater to move suddenly to compensate for the displacement. Most tsunamis are caused by earthquakes on the seafloor or induced by volcanic eruptions that suddenly boil or displace large amounts of water. The locations of earthquakes and volcanoes are controlled by *plate tectonics.* Therefore, the chapter starts with a review of the basic elements of the plate tectonic theory. Giant submarine landslides where huge masses of material suddenly slide down underwater slopes have initiated other tsunamis. Geologists have shown that it is even possible that gases dissolved in ices on the seafloor may suddenly be released, forming a huge bubble that erupts upward displacing the surface, generating a tsunami. The most catastrophic tsunamis in the geological record have been generated when asteroids or meteorites hit Earth in the oceans, displacing huge amounts of water in an instant, forming waves that could reach thousands of feet in height.

## Plate Tectonics and Tsunami Generation

The Earth formed about 4.5 billion years ago during the condensation of the *solar nebula,* a swirling mass of dust, gas, protoplanets, and the Sun, which left our present solar system with eight main planets and many smaller bodies (including Pluto, formerly regarded as a planet) circling the Sun. During its formation, the Earth was differentiated into several layers, including an outermost layer called the crust that is 3–50 miles (5–70 km) thick. This is followed by the mantle, a solid rocky layer extending 1,800 miles (2,900 km) beneath the surface. Then these are succeeded by the outer core, a molten metallic layer extending 3,200 miles (5,100 km) deep, and the inner core, a solid metallic layer extending 3,950 miles (6,370 km) to the center of the Earth.

Plate tectonics, a relatively new theory in the Earth Sciences, proposes that the outer shells of the Earth are divided into many different rigid plates that are all moving with respect to each other. This outer rigid layer is known as the *lithosphere,* which comes from the Greek word for "rigid rock sphere." The lithosphere ranges from 45–100 miles (75–150 km) thick. It floats on a denser, but partially molten and weaker, layer of rock in the upper mantle known as the *asthenosphere* (Greek for "weak sphere"). It is the weakness of this layer that allows the plates on the surface of the Earth to move around.

The tectonic plates are rigid and do not break, bend, or otherwise deform internally when they move, but only deform along their edges. The edges of plates are therefore where most mountain ranges are located and where most of the world's earthquakes occur and active volcanoes are located. Most tsunamis are generated by tectonic earthquake or volcanic activity along plate boundaries.

There are only three fundamental types of plate boundaries. *Divergent boundaries* are where two plates move apart, creating a void that is typically filled by new magma that solidifies to form oceanic crust that wells up to fill the progressively opening hole. Convergent boundaries are where two plates move toward each other, resulting in one plate sliding beneath the other when a dense oceanic plate is involved, or collision and deformation, when continental plates are involved. Lines of volcanoes, known as *volcanic arcs,* form above these sinking plates, resting on the edge of the overriding plate. *Transform boundaries* form where two plates slide past each other, such as along the San Andreas Fault in California.

Where plates diverge, *seafloor spreading* produces new oceanic crust, as volcanic *basalt* pours out of the depths of the Earth, filling the gaps generated by the moving plates. Examples of where this can be seen on the surface include Iceland along the Rekjanes Ridge. Beneath the Rekjanes and other oceanic ridges, magma rises from depth in the mantle and forms chambers filled with magma just below the crest of the ridges. The magma in these chambers erupts out through cracks in the roof of the chambers and forms extensive *lava* flows on the surface. As the two different plates on either side of the magma chamber move

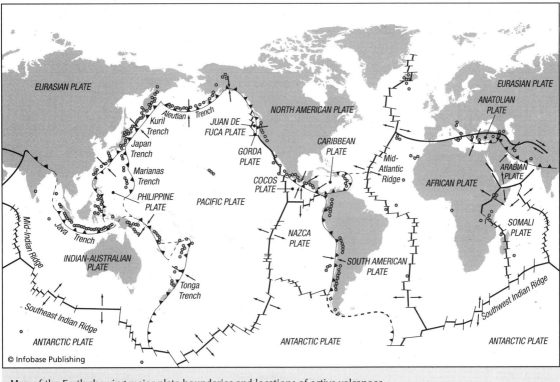

Map of the Earth showing major plate boundaries and locations of active volcanoes

apart, these lava flows continuously fill in the gap between the diverging plates, creating new oceanic crust.

In a process called subduction, oceanic lithosphere is being destroyed by sinking back into the mantle at the deep ocean trenches. As the oceanic slabs go down, they bend and crack and break, generating many large earthquakes along convergent boundaries. These earthquakes create the majority of tsunamis that affect coastal regions of the planet. The subducted plates also get heated to higher temperatures as they reach deep into the mantle and cause rock melts, or magmas, to be generated, which then move upward to intrude the overlying plate. Since subduction zones are long narrow zones where large plates are being subducted into the mantle, the melting produces a long line of volcanoes above the down-going plate and forms a volcanic arc. Depending on what the overriding plate is made of, this arc may be built on either a continental or on an oceanic plate. Volcanic eruptions along convergent plate boundaries have also generated a large number of tsunamis.

Convergent plate boundaries are often associated with great earthquakes, where huge masses of land, hundreds of miles long, resting above the subducting plate are suddenly thrust upward, displacing the seafloor and vast amounts of water in the oceans above. Therefore, most of the destructive tsunamis in history have been generated at convergent plate boundaries. Divergent plate boundaries are typically associated with smaller earthquakes and smaller displacement of the seafloor and therefore typically are not the sites of tsunami generation. Transform boundaries rarely displace the seafloor in the vertical direction and thus are also not typically associated with tsunami generation.

## Earthquake-Induced Tsunamis

Tectonic plate movement causes earthquakes. Nearly all of the convergent plate boundaries on the planet are located in the oceans because

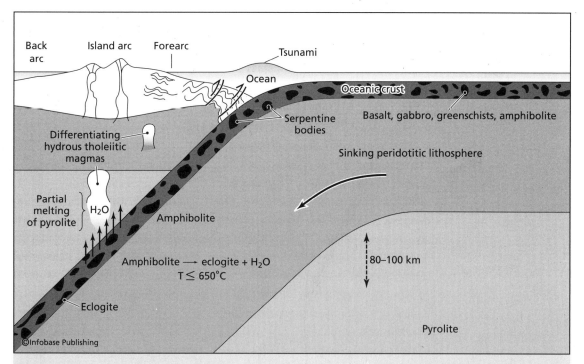

Cross section view of an island arc system, where a subducting oceanic plate is pushed beneath an overriding plate. Magma released from the subducting plate intrudes into the overriding plate forming the magmatic arc. The back-arc region lies between the arc and a distant continent, whereas the forearc region lies between the arc and the subduction zone trench. Many of history's worst tsunamis have been caused by thrust faults in forearc regions that suddenly uplifted huge sections of the forearc, displacing vast amounts of water that organizes into deep-ocean tsunamis.

the bending of oceanic plates into subduction zones causes the surface of the crust to be pulled down to several miles depth. Most of the largest earthquakes occur along convergent plate boundaries. Larger earthquakes are generally associated with larger amounts of crust suddenly moving at one time. Therefore, convergent plate boundaries represent the places where the largest sudden movements of sections of the seafloor can occur. The sudden movement of the seafloor must move huge volumes of water, and this displacement of water is what causes many tsunamis.

Earthquakes that strike offshore or near the coast have generated most of the world's tsunamis. In general, the larger the earthquake, the larger the tsunami, but this is not always the case. Earthquakes that have large amounts of vertical displacement of the seafloor result in larger tsunamis than earthquakes that have predominantly horizontal movements of the seafloor. This difference is approximately a factor of 10, probably because earthquakes with vertical displacements are much more effective at pushing large volumes of water upward or downward, generating tsunami. Another factor that influences how large a tsunami may be that is generated by an earthquake is the speed at which the seafloor breaks during the earthquake. Slower ruptures tend to produce larger tsunamis. In general, earthquakes with a magnitude of 6.5 or greater, with a shallow *focus* or place of rupture, are required to generate a tsunami.

*Tsunami earthquakes* are a special category of earthquakes that generate tsunamis that are unusually large for the earthquake's magnitude. Tsunami earthquakes are generated by large displacements that occur along faults near the seafloor. Most are generated on steeply dipping seafloor surface–penetrating faults that have vertical displacements along them during the earthquake, displacing the maximum amount of water. These types of earthquakes also frequently cause large submarine landslides or *slumps,* which also generate tsunamis. In contrast to tsunamis generated by vertical slip on vertical faults, which cause a small region to experience a large uplift, other tsunamis are generated by movement on very shallowly dipping faults. These are capable of causing large regions to experience minor uplift, displacing large volumes of water and generating a tsunami. Some of the largest tsunamis may have been generated by earthquake-induced slumps along convergent tectonic plate boundaries. In 1896, a huge 75-foot (23-m) tsunami was generated by an earthquake-induced submarine slump in Sanriku, Japan, killing 26,000 people in the wave. Another famous tsunami gen-

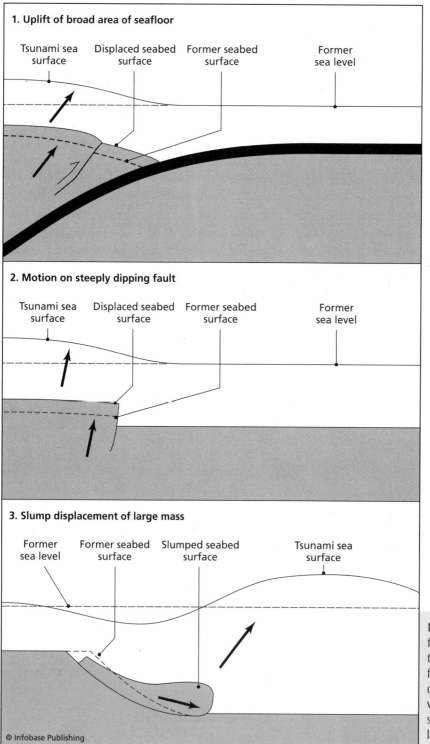

**1. Uplift of broad area of seafloor**

Tsunami sea surface    Displaced seabed surface    Former seabed surface    Former sea level

**2. Motion on steeply dipping fault**

Tsunami sea surface    Displaced seabed surface    Former seabed surface    Former sea level

**3. Slump displacement of large mass**

Former sea level    Former seabed surface    Slumped seabed surface    Tsunami sea surface

© Infobase Publishing

Diagram showing types of faults that generate large tsunamis, including 1) thrust faults in forearc regions of convergent margins, 2) vertical displacement of the seafloor, and 3) slumping of large blocks into the water.

erated by a slump from an earthquake was the 1946 wave that hit Hilo, Hawaii. This tsunami was 50 feet (15 m) high, killed 150 people, and caused about $25 million in damage to Hilo and surrounding areas. The amazing thing was that it was generated by an earthquake-induced slump off Unimak Island in the Aleutian chain of Alaska four-and-one-half hours earlier. This tsunami traveled at 500 MPH (800 km/hr) across the Pacific, hitting Hawaii without warning.

Another potent kind of tsunami-generating earthquake occurs along subduction zones. Sometimes, when certain kinds of earthquakes strike in this environment, the entire *forearc* region above the subducting plate may snap upward by up to a few tens of feet, displacing a huge amount of water. The devastating 2004 Indian Ocean tsunami was generated by motion of a 600-mile- (1,000-km-) long segment of the forearc of the Sumatra arc and subduction zone. The tsunami generated during the 1964 magnitude 9.2 Alaskan earthquake also formed a tsunami of this sort, and it caused numerous deaths and extensive destruction in places as far away as California.

More rarely, tsunamis may be generated by horizontal movements along vertical *strike-slip faults.* It is more difficult to form tsunami by motion on strike-slip faults because the sideways motion on these faults does not cause the water surface to be directly disturbed.

## Volcanic Eruption–Induced Tsunamis

Some of the largest recorded tsunamis have been generated by volcanic eruptions. These may be associated with the collapse of volcanic slopes, debris- and ashflows that displace large amounts of water, or submarine eruptions that explosively displace water above the volcano. It is estimated that 20 percent of volcanic-induced tsunamis form when volcanic ash or *pyroclastic* flows hit the ocean, displacing large amounts of water, and 20 percent form from earthquakes associated with the eruption. About 15 percent result from eruptions beneath the water and 7 percent result from collapse of the volcano and landslides into the sea. The remaining causes are not known. The most famous volcanic eruption–induced tsunami includes the series of huge waves generated by the eruption of Krakatau in 1883, which reached run-up heights of 120 feet (37 m) and killed 36,500 people. The number of people who perished in the eruption of Santorini in 1650 b.c.e. is not known, but the toll must have been huge. The waves reached 800 feet (244 m) high on islands close to the volcanic vent. Flood deposits have been found 300 feet (91 m) above sea level in parts of the Mediterranean Sea and extend as far as

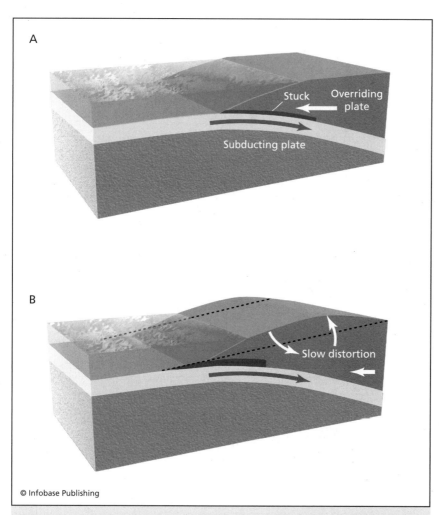

A

Stuck  Overriding plate

Subducting plate

B

Slow distortion

© Infobase Publishing

*(this page and opposite page)* Most devastating tsunamis, including the 2004 Indian Ocean tsunami, are generated by forearc earthquakes. The four block diagrams show the typical sequence of events that causes forearc earthquakes and tsunamis: (A) shows the subduction zone and forearc, where the overriding plate becomes attached or stuck to the subducting plate; (B) shows the slow sequential distortion of the forearc region, until just before breaking point; (C) illustrates the sudden movement of a large section of the forearc during an earthquake, displacing huge amounts of seawater into giant waves near the earthquake source; and (D) shows how the giant waves and displaced water organize into a massive tsunami that moves away from the earthquake source.

200 miles (320 km) southward up the Nile River. Several geologists suggest that these were formed from a tsunami generated by the eruption of Santorini. The floods from this eruption may also, according to some scientists, account for legends such as the great biblical flood, the part-

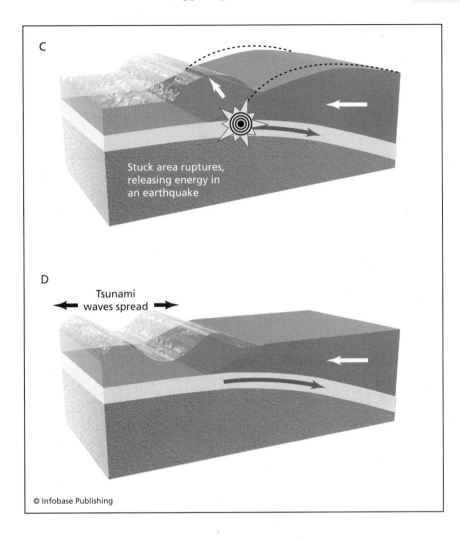

ing of the Red Sea during the exodus of the Israelites from Egypt, and the destruction of the Minoan civilization on the island of Crete.

The specific mechanisms by which volcanic eruptions can form tsunamis are diverse but number less than a dozen. Perhaps the most common is from earthquakes associated with volcanism. Many volcanic eruptions are accompanied by swarms of moderate-sized earthquakes, and some of these may be large enough to trigger tsunamis. This is especially true in cases of volcanoes built at convergent margins that are partway under sea level, such as Mount Vesuvius in Italy. The 79 C.E. eruption of Vesuvius was associated with many earthquake-induced tsunamis, some being triggered before the main eruption and others during and after the eruption.

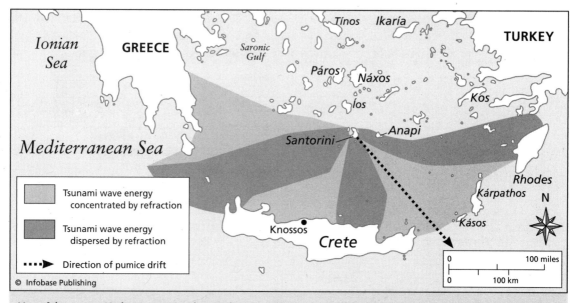

Map of the eastern Mediterranean Sea showing location of Santorini and the areas most affected by the massive eruption in 1650 B.C.E.

When pyroclastic flows or *nuée ardents* surge down the slopes of volcanoes they may eventually reach the ocean where they displace water and spread laterally. Some pyroclastic flows are less dense than water and produce layers of ash and pumice that ride over the ocean surface, whereas others are denser than seawater and can suddenly displace large volumes of water, producing a tsunami. In these cases, the larger the flow, the larger the resulting tsunami. Some pyroclastic flows are dense and continue to flow in a surgelike manner on the seafloor, pushing a wall of water ahead of the flow, thus generating a tsunami. The August 26, 1883, eruption of Krakatau in Indonesia generated a 33-foot- (10-m-) high tsunami by such an undersea surge of a pyroclastic flow, whereas the March 5, 1871, eruption of Ruang volcano, also in Indonesia, produced an 82-foot- (25-m-) high tsunami by this mechanism.

Submarine eruptions in shallow water can generate tsunami by displacing water when the volcano erupts. When the water is deeper than about 1,650 feet (503 m), the weight of the water is so great that it suppresses the formation of surface waves. This is fortunate, since there are many volcanic eruptions along the 8,900-foot- (2,700-m-) deep *mid-ocean ridge*s, and if each of these generated a tsunami, the coastal zone on most continents would be constantly plagued with tsunamis. When submarine eruptions expose the magma chamber of a volcano to seawater, larger tsunamis result from the sudden steam explosion as the cold seawater vaporizes as it touches the extremely hot magma. An explosion of this sort generated the deadly 1883 tsunami from the eruption of Krakatau in Indonesia, when a steam explosion formed a 130-foot- (40-m-) high tsunami that killed tens of thousands of people.

One of the most catastrophic ways to suddenly bring large volumes of seawater into contact with a magma chamber is through the formation of a *caldera,* where the top of the volcanic complex suddenly collapses into the magma chamber, forming a large depression on the surface. If the volcano is located at or near sea level, ocean waters can suddenly rush into the depression, where they will encounter the hot magma and form giant steam eruptions. There are many volcanoes around the Pacific rim that have formed caldera structures and many appear to have generated tsunamis. The most famous is the tsunami associated with the formation of the caldera on Krakatau in 1883, in which the tsunami devastated the Sunda Strait, killing thousands of people. Another example of a tsunami generated by seawater rushing into a collapsing caldera is Mount Ritter in Papua New Guinea. On March 13, 1888, a 1.5-mile- (2.5-km-) wide caldera collapsed beneath the volcano and the sea rushed in, generating a 50-foot- (15-m-) high tsunami that swept local shores. The actual amount of seawater displaced in a tsunami formed by caldera collapse is small, typically many orders of magnitude smaller than the amount displaced during large earthquakes. Tsunamis associated with caldera collapse tend not to travel very far, but to decay in height quickly, according to the inverse of the square root of the distance from the source.

Tsunamis can be generated from volcanoes during collapse of the slopes and formation of landslides and debris avalanches that move into the ocean. Most tsunamis generated by the collapse of slopes of volcanoes are small, localized, and very directional in that they propagate directly away from the landslide or debris avalanche and fade rapidly in other directions. Many volcanoes around the Pacific rim have steep slopes near the sea and pose hazards for tsunamis generated by slope collapse. Some of these can be quite powerful locally, as shown by the example of Mount Unzen in Japan. On May 21, 1792, a large debris avalanche roared off the slope of the volcano, traveled four miles (6.5 km), and hit the seawater of the Ariake Sea. This displaced enough water to generate a tsunami with run-up heights of up to 170 feet (52 m) along a

50-mile- (77-km-) long section of the Shimabara Peninsula coast, killing 14,524 people, destroying 6,000 homes, and sinking 1,650 ships. Other volcanic islands, such as Hawaii and the Canary Islands, pose a different kind of landslide threat, in which large sections of the volcano collapse forming giant undersea landslides, with associated tsunamis.

A final way that volcanoes can form tsunamis is through lateral blasts, or sideways eruptions, from the volcano. The most famous lateral blast from a volcano is the well-documented 1980 eruption of Mount Saint Helens, but this was far from the ocean and did not generate a tsunami. Some volcanoes have a tendency to erupt sideways. One of these is Taal in the Philippines where at least five lateral blasts have occurred in the past 250 years, each generating a deadly tsunami.

A number of other tsunamis have been generated from mass wasting processes on volcanic slopes, but these can generally be classified as being caused by landslides or one of the mechanisms from movement of lava discussed in this section. Mudflows and *lahars* have generated many tsunamis and lava flows, if large and fast enough, can also generate tsunamis. Most of these only generate small, localized, and strongly directional tsunamis.

## Landslide-Induced Tsunamis

Many tsunamis are generated by landslides that displace large amounts of water. These may be from rockfalls and other debris that fall off cliffs into the water, such as the huge avalanche that triggered a 200-foot- (60-m-) high tsunami in Lituya Bay, Alaska. Submarine landslides tend to be larger than avalanches that originate above the waterline and have generated some of the largest tsunamis on record. Many submarine landslides are earthquake-induced; others are triggered by storm events or increases in pressure on the sediments of the continental shelf induced by rises in sea level. A deeper water column above the sediments on a shelf or slope environment can significantly increase the pressure in the pores of these sediments, causing them to become unstable and slide downslope. After the last glacial retreat 6,000–10,000 years ago, sea levels have risen by 320–425 feet (98–130 m), which has greatly increased the pore pressure on continental slope sediments around the world. This increase in pressure is thought to have initiated many submarine landslides, including the large Storegga slides from 7,950 years ago off the coast of Norway.

Tsunamis are suspected of being landslide-induced when the earthquake is not large enough to produce the observed size of the asso-

Photo of Liyuya Bay in August 1958, showing landslide and tsunami damage. Note the absence of trees around the shoreline, which were washed away by the tsunami. *(USGS)*

ciated tsunami. Many areas beneath the sea are characterized by steep slopes, including areas along most continental margins, around islands, and along convergent plate boundaries. Sediments near deep-sea trenches are often saturated in water and close to the point of failure, where the slope gives out and collapses, causing the pile of sediments to suddenly slide down to deeper water depths. When an earthquake strikes these areas large parts of the submarine slopes may give out simultaneously, displacing water and generating a tsunami. The 1964 magnitude 9.2 earthquake in Alaska generated more than 20 tsunamis, which were responsible for most of the damage and death from this earthquake.

Some steep submarine slopes that are not characterized by earthquakes may also be capable of generating huge tsunamis. Recent studies along the East Coast of North America, off the coast of Atlantic City, New Jersey, have revealed significant tsunami hazards. Its submarine geology consists of a several-thousand-feet-thick pile of unconsolidated sediments on the continental slope. These sediments are so porous and saturated with water that the entire slope is on the verge of collapsing under its own weight. A storm or minor earthquake may be enough to trigger a giant submarine landslide in this area, possibly generating a tsunami that could sweep across the beaches of Long Island, New Jersey, Delaware, and much of the rest of the East Coast of the United States.

Storms are capable of generating submarine landslides even if the storm waves do not reach and disrupt the seafloor. Large storms are associated with *storm surges* that form a mound of water in front of the storm that may sometimes reach 20–32 feet (6–10 m) in height. As the storm surge moves onto the continental shelf, it is often preceded by a drop in sea level caused by a drop in air pressure, so the storm surge may be associated with large pressure changes on the seafloor and in the pores of unconsolidated sediments. A famous example of a storm surge–induced tsunami is the catastrophic event in Tokyo, Japan, on September 1, 1923. On this day, a powerful typhoon swept across Tokyo, followed that evening by a huge submarine landslide and earthquake that generated a 36-foot- (11-m-) tall tsunami that swept across

Tokyo, killing 143,000 people. Surveys of the seabed after the tsunami revealed that large sections had slid to sea, deepening the bay in many places by 300–650 feet (91–198 m), and locally by as much as 1,300 feet (396 m). Similar storm-induced submarine slides can be known from many continental slopes and delta environments, including the Mississippi delta in the Gulf of Mexico and the coast of Central America.

Submarine slides are part of a larger group of processes that can move material downslope on the seafloor and includes other related processes such as slumps, debris flows, grain flows, and turbidity currents. Submarine slumps are a type of sliding slope failure in which a downward and outward rotational movement of the slope occurs along a concave up slip surface. This produces either a singular or a series of rotated blocks, each with the original seafloor surface tilted in the same direction. Slumps can move large amounts of material short distances in short times and are capable of generating tsunamis. Debris flows involve the downslope movement of unconsolidated sediment and water, most of which is coarser than sand. Some debris flows begin as slumps, but then continue to flow downslope as debris flows. They fan out and come to rest when they emerge out of submarine canyons onto flat *abyssal plains* on the deep seafloor. Rates of movement in debris flows vary from several feet per year to several hundred MPH. Debris flows are commonly shaped like a tongue with numerous ridges and depressions. Large debris flows can suddenly move large volumes of sediment, so are also capable of generating tsunami. *Turbidity currents* are sudden movements of water-saturated sediments that move downhill under the force of gravity. These form when water-saturated sediment on a shelf or shallow water setting is disturbed by a storm, earthquake, or some other mechanism that triggers the sliding of the sediment downslope. The sediment-laden sediment/water mixture then moves rapidly downslope as a density current and may travel tens or even hundreds of miles at tens of miles per hour until the slope decreases and the velocity of current decreases. As the velocity of the current decreases, the ability of the current to hold coarse material in suspension decreases. The current drops first its coarsest load, then progressively finer material as the current decreases further. Turbidity currents do not usually generate tsunamis, but many are associated with slumps and debris flows that may generate tsunamis. However, some turbidity flows are so massive that they may form tsunamis.

Volcanic *hot spot* islands in the middle of some oceans have a long record of producing tsunamis from submarine landslides. These islands include Hawaii in the Pacific Ocean, the Cape Verde Islands in the North Atlantic, and Reunion in the Indian Ocean. The shape of many of these islands bears the telltale starfish shape with cuspate scars indicating the locations of old curved landslide surfaces. On average, a significant tsunami is generated somewhere in the world every 100 years from the collapse and submarine landside from a midocean volcanic island. These islands are volcanically active, and lava flows move across the surface and then cool and crystallize quickly as the lava enters the water. This causes the islands to grow upward as very steep-sided columns, whose sides are prone to massive collapse and submarine sliding. Many volcanic islands are built up with a series of volcanic growth periods followed by massive submarine landslides, effectively widening the island as it grows. However, island growth by deposition of a series of volcanic flows over older landslide scars causes the island to be unstable—the old landslide scars are prone to later slip since they are weak surfaces and the added stress of the new material piled on top of them makes them unstable. Other processes may also contribute to making these surfaces and the parts of the island above them unstable. For instance, on the Hawaiian Islands volcanic *dikes* have intruded along some old landslide scars, which can reduce the strength across the old surfaces by large amounts. Some parts of Hawaii are moving away from the main parts of the island by up to 0.5–4 inches (1–10 cm) per year by the intrusion of volcanic dikes along old slip surfaces. Also, many landslide surfaces are characterized by accumulations of weathered material and blocks of rubble that under the additional weight of new volcanic flows can help to reduce the friction on the old slip surfaces, aiding the generation of new landslides. Therefore, as the islands grow, they are prone to additional large submarine slides that may generate tsunamis.

Simon Day, a British geologist, describes some new computer models of the potential tsunami effects from giant landslides that may one day be generated from oversteepened coastal cliffs in the volcanic Cape Verde and Canary Islands. These island chains are located in the eastern Atlantic off the coast of western Africa and were constructed from hot spot volcanism (i.e., not associated with the mid-ocean ridge or island arcs). The islands have very steep western slopes, and Simon Day has completed fieldwork that suggests that these cliffs are unstable. He and his colleagues have suggested that if new *magma* enters the volcanic islands, it may heat the groundwater in the fractures in the rock, creating enough pressure to induce the giant cliffs to collapse. Any landslides generated from such an anticipated collapse would have the potential to generate giant tsunamis that could sweep the shores of the Atlantic. The wave height will diminish with distance from the Cape Verde Islands, but the effects on the shores of eastern North America, the Caribbean, and eastern South America are expected to be devastating if this event ever occurs. The waves will probably also wrap around the Cape Verde Islands, hitting the British mainland and the western coast of Africa with smaller, but still damaging, waves, as described in the following sidebar.

## PREDICTION OF A FUTURE ATLANTIC TSUNAMI FROM COLLAPSE OF CUMBRE VIEJA VOLCANO, CANARY ISLANDS

Simon Day, a British geologist working at the Benfield Hazard Research Center at University College London, with coworker Simon Ward from the University of California, Santa Cruz, have developed a frightening model for what may happen in the predicted future collapse of a volcanic island in the Canary Islands off the coast of western Africa. Writing in a report "Issues in Risk Science" published in 2003, they outlined the following scenario:

"Lateral collapses of oceanic island volcanoes in the Canary and Cape Verde archipelagos and other Atlantic island groups are predicted to produce giant tsunami. Although the long-term frequency of these events is low, the likely consequences are so severe as to make this a significant long-term hazard, perhaps more significant on thousand to hundred-thousand year timescales than asteroid impact-triggered tsunami. Furthermore, there are indications of a possible impending collapse on at least one island volcano in the Atlantic. Of most relevance to volcano collapse generated tsunami hazards in the Atlantic is a model of a future collapse of the Cumbre Vieja volcano on La Palma. A model of a landslide with a volume of 120 cubic miles (500 cubic km) and a wedge shaped geometry based upon the geometry of the volcano, traveling downslope for 9 miles (15 km) as a sliding block at high speed before disintegrating into a debris avalanche that then spreads out over the ocean floor for 37 miles (60 km) from the island. Rather than consisting of a single wave, the resulting tsunami develops into a train of a dozen or more very large waves. Notable features of the model are the very wide arc (of the waves) to the north, west, and south of the Canaries where very large tsunami amplitudes are predicted to be present, even in deep water where typical earthquake-generated tsunami amplitudes are only a 3–6 feet (1–2 m); the buildup of wave amplitudes to as much as 130–160 feet (40–50 m) as the waves move into shallow water offshore from the coasts of Greenland, North America, the Caribbean, and northern Brazil, 2,500 miles (4,000 km) or more from the Canaries, and the even larger wave amplitudes developed on many coasts closer to the source landslide on La Palma. Other models produce a range of results with variations in wave heights by a factor of two or so, but still with very large (65 feet [20 m] or more) wave amplitudes in coastal waters at trans-ocean distances."

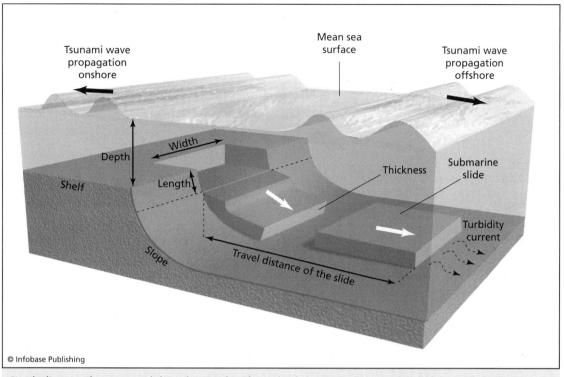

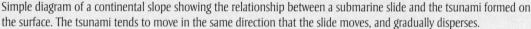

Simple diagram of a continental slope showing the relationship between a submarine slide and the tsunami formed on the surface. The tsunami tends to move in the same direction that the slide moves, and gradually disperses.

The characteristics of tsunamis generated by landslides depend on the amount of material that moves downslope, the depth that the material moves from and to, and the speed at which the slide moves. Tsunamis generated by submarine landslides are usually quite different from those generated by other processes such as displacements of the seafloor caused by earthquakes. Submarine slides move material in one direction, and the resulting tsunami tends also to be more focused in slide-induced events than from other triggering mechanisms. Tsunamis produced by submarine slides are characterized by a wave located above the slide that moves offshore parallel to the direction the slide has moved. A complementary wave is produced that moves in the opposite direction, upslope and toward shore.

Tsunamis resulting from submarine slides also have wave shapes that are different from waves generated by earthquake-induced displacement of the seafloor. Most slide-induced tsunamis have a first wave with a small crest, followed by a deep trough that may be three times deeper than the height of the first wave. The next wave will have the height of the trough, but may change into several waves with time. The large height difference between the first wave and the succeeding trough leads tsunamis generated by landslides to often have greater run-up heights than tsunamis generated by other mechanisms. Slide-induced tsunamis also differ from other tsunamis in that they start with slow velocities as the submarine slide forms, then must accelerate as they take form. Therefore, the arrival time of slide-induced tsunamis at shore locations is later than expected. The *wavelengths* of tsunamis from submarine slides are typically 0.5–6 miles (1–10 km) and the periods range from 1 to 5 minutes. The period may increase as the area of the slide increases and the slope of the seafloor decreases. Submarine landslides rarely move faster than 160 feet per second (50 m/sec), whereas the resulting tsunamis quickly accelerate to 325–650 feet per second (100–200 m/sec). The characteristics of tsunamis produced by submarine slides are therefore quite different from tsunamis produced by other mechanisms.

## Natural Gas and Gas Hydrate Eruption–Induced Tsunamis

The *continental shelves* and slopes around most continents are the sites of deposition of thick piles of sediments. River deltas such as that of the Mississippi may add even more sediments to these environments, in some cases forming piles of sediment that are 10 miles (16 km) thick, deposited over many millions of years. Natural gas is produced in submarine sediments by the anaerobic decay of organic matter that becomes buried with the sediments. The gas produced by the decay of these organic particles may escape or become trapped within the sediments. When the gas gets trapped between the pore spaces of the sediments, it causes the pressure to build up in a process called underconsolidation. These pressures can become very large and even be greater than the pressure exerted by the weight of the overlying water, which is called "hydrostatic pressure." When the gas pressure within a layer or larger section of sediments on the continental shelves and slopes becomes greater than the hydrostatic pressure, the sediments on the slope are on the verge of failure, so that any small disturbance could cause a massive submarine landslide, in turn inducing a tsunami.

Decaying organic matter on the seafloor releases large volumes of gas, such as methane. Under some circumstances, including cold water at deep depths, these gases may coagulate, forming gels called

## GAS HYDRATES AND
## FUTURE ENERGY RESOURCES

The hydrocarbon energy resources most widely used by industrial nations are rapidly running out. Geologists know the location of approximately 600 billion barrels of oil; estimates for total global oil reserves are 1,500–3,000 billion barrels. There may be unknown reserves in small deposits, but not tars, tar sands, and oil shales, which must be heated and extensively processed to make them useful and thus are very expensive. Humans have used up about 500 billion barrels and now use 30 million barrels of oil a year. Therefore, known reserves will last 20–50–100 years at the most. Oil is running out and is becoming an increasingly powerful political weapon. The oil-rich nations can effectively hold the rest of the world hostage, because we have become so dependent on oil. Future energy sources may include nuclear fuels, solar, hydroelectric, geothermal, biomass, wind, tidal, and, perhaps most promising, gas hydrates.

Gas hydrates, or clathrates, are solid, icelike water-gas mixtures that form at cold temperatures (40–43°F [4–6°C]) and pressures above 50 atmospheres. Large parts of the ocean floor are covered by deposits of gas hydrates. They form on deep marine continental margins and in polar continental regions, often below the seafloor. These solid icelike substances are made of cases of ice molecules enclosing gas molecules that are typically methane, but may include ethane, butane, propane, carbon dioxide, and hydrogen sulfides. The methane is formed by anaerobic bacterial degradation of organic material. Gas hydrates have recently been recognized as a huge global energy resource, with reserves estimated to be at least twice that of known fossil fuel deposits. Gas hydrates form at high pressures and cold temperatures, and extracting them from the deep ocean without releasing huge amounts of $CO_2$ into the atmosphere may be difficult.

It is estimated that gas hydrates may contain twice the amount of carbon of all fossil fuel deposits on the planet and, as such, represent a huge, virtually untapped potential source of energy. However, the gases expand by more than 150 times the volume of the hydrates, they are located deep in the ocean, and methane is a significant greenhouse gas. Therefore there are significant technical problems to overcome before gas hydrates are widely mined as an energy source, but they remain one of the most promising possible sources of energy to drive the needs of industrialized nations in the next century.

*gas hydrates,* as described in the sidebar above. It has recently been recognized that these gas hydrates occasionally spontaneously release their trapped gases in giant bubbles that rapidly erupt to the surface. Such catastrophic degassing of gas hydrates poses a significant tsunami threat to regions not previously thought to have a significant threat, such as along the East Coast of the United States.

## Other Tsunamis

Consider the tsunami generated by the massive landslide in Lituya Bay, Alaska, in 1958, as previously described. Now, consider what kind of tsunami may be generated by the impact of a giant asteroid with the Earth. These types of events do not happen very often and none are known from historical records, but when they do occur they are cataclysmic. Geologists are beginning to recognize deposits of impact-generated tsunamis and now estimate that they may reach 3,000 feet (914 m) in height. One such tsunami was generated about 66 million years ago by an impact that struck the shoreline of the Yucatán Peninsula, producing the Chicxulub impact structure. This impact produced a huge crater and sent a 3,000-foot- (914-m-) high tsunami around the Atlantic, devastating the Caribbean and the U.S. Gulf Coast. Subsequent fires and atmospheric dust that blocked the sun for several years killed off much of the planet's species, including the dinosaurs. Even relatively small meteorites that hit the ocean have the potential to generate significant tsunamis. It is estimated that a meteorite only 1,000 feet (305 m) in diameter would produce a tsunami seven feet (2 m) tall that could strongly affect coastal regions for 600 miles (1,000 km) around the impact site. There is about a 1 percent chance of impact-related tsunami events happening every 50 years.

Rarely, weather-related phenomena may also generate tsunami. In some special situations, large variations in atmospheric pressure, especially at temperate latitudes, can generate long-wavelength waves (tsunamis) that resonate, or become larger, in bays and estuaries. Although these types of tsunamis are not generated by displacement of the seafloor, they do have all the waveform characteristics of other tsunamis and are therefore classified as such.

## Conclusion

Tsunamis may be formed by a variety of mechanisms, but the most common generating mechanism is sudden displacement of the seafloor caused by earthquakes. Most tsunamogenic earthquakes are thrust-type along convergent margins, where large sections of the seafloor are suddenly pushed upward, forcing the overlying water to move aside, forming a tsunami. Volcanic eruptions may also generate tsunamis when the eruption occurs underwater and the magma causes the overlying water to suddenly boil in a steam eruption or when massive ash or lava falls into the ocean, displacing large amounts of water. Landslides and undersea slumps may also displace large amounts of water, forming tsunamis. Rarer mechanisms of tsunami generation include the sudden release of giant gas bubbles from the seafloor, weather-related atmospheric pressure gradients, and the impact of asteroids and meteorites in the oceans.

# 2

# Physics of Tsunami Movement

**W**itnessing the approach of a large tsunami can be one of the most awe-inspiring and deadly sights ever experienced by residents of low-lying coastal areas. Tsunamis are very different from normal storm- or wind-generated waves in that they have exceptionally long wavelengths, the distance between successive crests. Whereas most storm waves will rise, break, and dissipate most of their energy in the surf zone, tsunamis are characterized by a rapid rise of sea level that leads the wave to break at the shoreline, then to keep on rising or running up into the coastal zone for extended periods of time. This is related to the long wavelength of tsunamis. Most waves have distances between the crests of several hundreds of feet and rise and fall relatively quickly, as each wave crest passes. Tsunamis, however, may have distances between each wave crest of a hundred or even many hundreds of miles, so it may take half an hour, an hour, or more for the wave to stop its incessant and destructive rise into coastal areas and retreat into the sea, before the next crest of the tsunami train crashes into shore. Tsunamis are similar to normal wind-generated waves in that they have a series of wave crests separated by troughs. Like normal waves, after the first, typically hour-long wave sweeps through a coastal region and retreats, the tsunami event is not over. There will be a series of wave crests, sometimes with the second or third crest being the largest, that sweep into the coastal areas, each causing its own destruction. Many of the deaths reported from tsunami disasters are associated with the fact that many people do not understand this basic physical principle about tsunamis, and they rush to the coastal area after the first destructive wave to rescue injured people and become victims of the second or third crests' incursion onto the land. This chapter examines

- the basic physical principles of how tsunamis move, first in open ocean water and then in shallow water
- the awesome forces that are released when the tsunami crashes into and runs up through the coastal environment, then retreats to the sea dragging everything it can with it during its escape
- the specific hazards associated with the different phases of the tsunami.

## Movement in Open Ocean

Tsunamis are waves with exceptionally large distances between individual crests that move like other waves across the ocean. The waves of tsunamis are described using the terms of the regular geometrically repeating pattern of waves. Waves in a series are called a *wave train,* with regularly repeating crests and troughs. Wavelength is the distance between crests, wave height is the vertical distance from the crest to the bottom of the trough, and *amplitude* is one-half of the wave height. The *wave period* is the time between the passage of two successive crests. Most tsunamis have wave periods of 1.6–33 minutes. Most ocean waves have wavelengths of 300 feet (91 m) or less. Tsunamis are exceptional in that they have wavelengths that can be 120 miles (200 km) or greater. The particle motion in deepwater waves follows roughly circular paths, where particles move approximately in a circle, and return back to their starting position after the wave passes. The amount of circular motion decreases gradually with depth, until a depth that equals one-half of the wavelength. At this depth all motion associated with the passage of the wave stops, and the water beneath this point experiences no effect from the passage of the wave above. This depth is known as the *wave base.* The movement of deepwater waves is therefore associated with the transfer of energy, but not the transfer of water from place to place.

The particle motion of individual molecules of water during the passage of tsunamis is elliptical, similar to the circular motion of other deepwater waves as described in the following sidebar. The motion of any particles during the passage of the waves follows elliptical paths, first forward, down, then up and back to near the starting point during the passage of individual wave crests. The passage of deepwater tsunamis is therefore associated with the movement and transportation of individual particles. The reason that particle paths in tsunamis are elliptical and other deepwater waves produce circular motion is that tsunamis have such long wavelengths that the oceans depth of 2–3 miles (3–5 km) is less than the wave base. Tsunamis therefore travel as shallow-water waves across the open ocean where the water depth is less than the wave base, and thus they feel some frictional effect from the ocean bottom. This friction distorts the preferred circular particle paths into the elliptical paths that are observed in tsunamis. The end result is that tsunamis are associated with motion of the entire water column during passage, whereas wind-generated waves only

## THE PHYSICS OF WIND-BLOWN WAVES

Normal ocean waves are geometrically regular and repeating undulations on the surface of water that move and transport energy from one place to another. Waves are generated by winds that blow across the water surface, and the frictional drag of the wind on the surface transfers energy from the air to the sea, where it is expressed as waves. The waves may travel great distances across entire ocean basins, and they may be thought of as energy in motion. This energy is released or transferred to the shoreline when the waves crash on the beach. It is this energy that is able to move entire beaches and erode cliffs grain-by-grain, slowly changing the appearance of the beach environment.

When waves are generated by winds over deepwater, often from distant storms, they develop a characteristic spacing and height known as the wavelength and height or amplitude. The wave crest is the highest part of the wave, and the wave trough is the low point between waves. Wavelength is the distance between successive crests or troughs, the wave height is the vertical distance between troughs and crests, and amplitude is one-half of the wave height. *Wave fronts* are (imaginary) lines drawn parallel to the wave crests, and the wave moves perpendicular to the wave fronts. The time (in seconds) that it takes successive wave crests to pass a point is known as the wave period.

The height, wavelength, and period of waves are determined by how strong the wind is that generates them, how long it blows for, and the distance over which the wind blows (known as the *fetch*). The longer and stronger and the greater the distance the wind blows, the longer the wavelength, the greater the wave height, and the longer the wave period.

It is important to remember that waves are energy in motion, and the water in the waves does not travel along with the waves. The motion of individual water particles as a wave passes is roughly a circular orbit that decreases in radius with depth below the wave. This type of motion can be experienced while sitting in waves in the ocean, where a person would feel themselves moving roughly up and down, or in a circular path, as the waves pass.

The motion of water particles in waves changes as the water depth decreases and the waves approach shore. At a depth equal to roughly one-half of the wavelength, the circular motion induced by the wave begins to feel the sea bottom, which exerts a frictional drag on the wave. This changes the circular particle paths to elliptical paths and causes the upper part of the wave to move ahead of the deeper parts. The wave becomes oversteepened and begins to break as the wave crashes into shore in the surf zone. In this surf zone, the water is actually moving forward causing the common erosion, transportation, and deposition of sand along beaches.

have motion down to the wave base, at a distance equal to half the wavelength.

Many tsunamis are different from regular waves in that they may have highly irregular wave train patterns. Some tsunamis have a high initial peak, followed by successively smaller wave crests, whereas other tsunamis have the highest crest located several crests behind the initial crest. The reasons for these differences are complex, but most are related to the nature of the triggering mechanism that formed the wave train. A splash or meteorite impact may create an initial large crest, whereas as undersea explosion may cause an initially small crest, followed by a larger one related to the interaction of the waves that fill the hole in the water column related to the explosion. There are many variables that contribute to the initial shape of the wave train, and each wave train needs to be examined separately to understand what caused its shape.

Different mechanisms of tsunami generation may form several sets of wave trains with different wavelengths. Longer wavelength wave trains travel at higher speeds than shorter wavelength wave trains, so the farther the tsunami travels from its source, the more spread out the waves of different wavelengths will become. This phenomenon is known as wave *dispersion.* The effect of dispersion is such that locations near the source will see complex waves where the short and long wavelength sets are superimposed and combine to make taller or shorter waves of each set as they crash onto shore. Locations more distant from the tsunami source will first experience the fast-traveling long-wavelength waves and then later be hit by the shorter wavelength (and period)

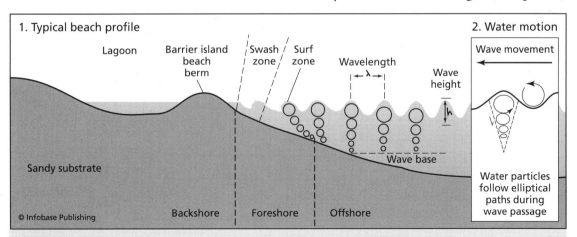

Definition of wave features including wavelength, height, and orbital paths followed by water as wave energy passes any point

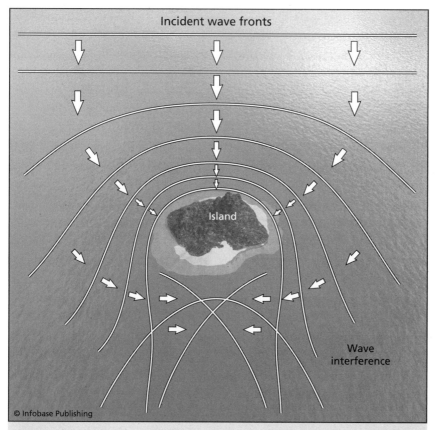

Diagram showing the effects of wave refraction of a tsunami or other waves around an island. As the wave fronts approach, the ones closer to the island begin to encounter shallow water and friction on the wave base slows them down while at the same time the parts of the wave far from the island continue to move at the initial speed. This causes the waves to bend around the island and meet behind the island where they interfere with each other before regrouping and continuing to move on. Where the waves interfere, crests can be added to other crests producing waves twice as high as the initial wave and troughs can be added to troughs producing deeper troughs. *(modified from Geological Survey of Canada)*

waves and then later be hit by the shorter wavelength (and period) waves. The time difference between these different sets becomes greater with increasing distance from the source.

When tsunamis are traveling across deep ocean water, their amplitudes are typically less than three feet (1 m), even though the wavelength may be more than 100 miles (160 km). A passenger on a ship would probably not even notice the largest of tsunamis if the ship was in the deep ocean (so the giant wave that sunk the leisure ship in the 1972 film *The Poseidon Adventure* must have been an entirely different creature, such as a *rogue wave*). Circular or elliptical paths that decrease in size with depth describe the motion of water in waves. All motion from the waves stops at a depth equal to one-half the distance of the wavelength. Since the wavelength of tsunamis is typically about 120 miles (200 km), movement associated with the passage of the waves can be felt to a depth of 60 miles (100 km), much greater than the depth of the oceans. Tsunamis therefore are felt at much greater depths than ordinary waves, and the normally still, deep-ocean environment will experience sudden elliptical motions, plus pressure differences, during their passage. Tsunami detectors on the deep ocean bottom use these effects to help warn coastal communities when tsunamis are approaching.

Since tsunamis are essentially shallow-water waves when they travel across the open ocean, they will experience different amounts of friction by different water depths and topographic features such as submerged mountains on the seafloor. The shallower the feature, the greater the friction, and the more it will slow the passage of the tsunami wave front above that feature. Tsunamis are like other waves in that when they encounter objects that slow their travel, they bend around the objects and are said to be refracted. *Refraction* of tsunamis is quite common in the Pacific and Indian Oceans. In the Pacific, this phenomenon is typically seen when waves generated along the Pacific subduction zones travel to the center of the ocean and get refracted around the islands of the Hawaiian chain. The bending of tsunami wave fronts around objects such as Hawaii can have two main effects on the wave energy. It can focus the energy in some locations where the wave fronts that bend around the object from either side merge and add together, or it can spread apart this energy and disperse it so that it is less intense. In the Pacific Ocean, the islands of Hawaii tend to focus the energy from earthquake-generated tsunamis that form along the western coasts of North and South America on the island of Japan. This is one reason that Japan has endured so many tsunami events in history. Japan must accommodate tsunamis generated locally by earthquakes and the shape of the seafloor in the Pacific focuses the energy from distant earthquake-generated tsunamis on Japan also. Tsunamis that are amplified from distant earthquakes are known as *teleseismic* tsunamis. An example of the opposite effect, the defocusing of seismic energy, is commonly afforded by the small island of Tahiti in French Polynesia. The seafloor topography of the Pacific commonly causes incoming tsunamis to be defocused or dispersed as the waves approach this island.

## Encounter with Shallow Water

Waves with long wavelengths travel faster than waves with short wave-lengths. Since the longer the wavelength the faster the wave in deep open water, tsunamis travel extremely fast across the ocean. Normal ocean waves travel at less than 55 MPH (90 km/hr), whereas many tsunamis travel at 375–600 MPH (800–900 km/hr), faster than most commercial airliners. The wave speeds slow down as the tsunamis encounter shallow water, typically to about 60–180 MPH (100–300 km/

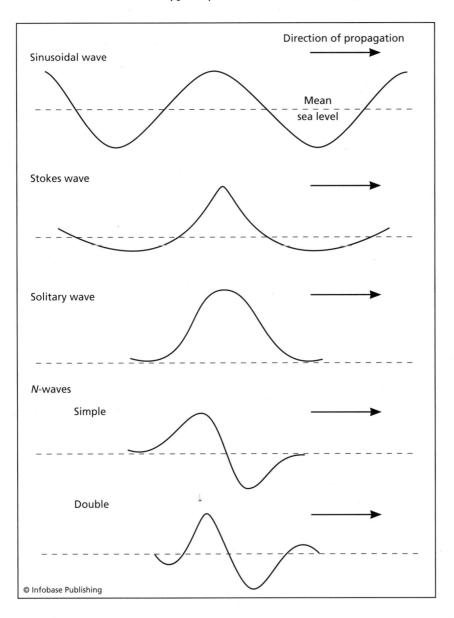

hr) across the continental shelves and about 22 MPH (36 km/hr) at the shore. This slowing of the wave speed as it begins to encounter shallow water causes the waves at the back of the train to be moving faster than those in the front. When this occurs the wave must become taller and narrower to accommodate the waves moving into the same space from behind. Thus, as the tsunami moves from being a deepwater wave into shallow waters, it becomes taller (larger amplitude), has a shorter distance between crests (shorter wavelength), and moves slower (velocity). In some cases, many of the crests will merge and the troughs will disappear during this process, producing a huge solitary wave, whose height from base to top is entirely above sea level.

When waves encounter shallow water, the friction of the seafloor along the base of the wave becomes greater, causing them to slow down dramatically and pile up on themselves as successive waves move toward shore. This causes the wave height or amplitude to increase dramatically, sometimes 10–150 feet (3–46 m) above the normal still waterline for tsunamis.

One of the main effects of the friction at the base of the tsunami as it enters shallow water is that the wave fronts tend to be strongly refracted so that they approach land at less than 10 degrees no matter what the original angle of approach to the shore was. This refraction

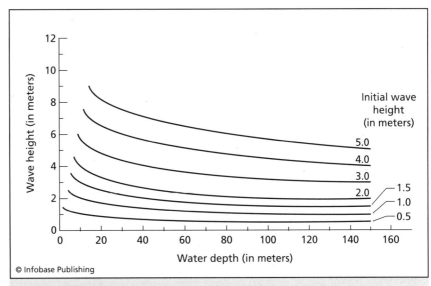

© Infobase Publishing

*(opposite page)* Idealized shapes of different kinds of waves
*(above)* Diagram showing how the wave heights of tsunamis are amplified as they move across the continental shelf from deep to shallow water (right to left)

occurs because the part of the wave that encounters shallow water first will be slowed down by the increased friction, whereas the other part of the wave still in deepwater will continue to move faster, until it catches up with the rest of the wave by being in the same water depth. This effect bends tsunamis, like other waves, so that they hit most shoreline areas nearly head-on. Seafloor topography very close to shore can modify this refraction and either focus the energy into specific locations or disperse it across the shoreline.

The friction at the base of the wave dissipates the energy from the tsunami. In most settings, the amount of dissipation is minor (less than 3 percent), but in some cases where the continental shelf areas are very wide and narrow, the dissipation can be significant enough to dramatically reduce the tsunami threat to the region. Such is the case for the section of the northeast seas of China (Yellow Sea, Bohai Sea, and related areas) where the water depth is quite shallow for many hundreds of miles, making the northeast coast of China much less susceptible to tsunami than the southeastern coast, where the shelf area is deeper and narrower. Much of the U.S. East Coast has a moderately wide and shallow shelf that is able to dissipate about 20 percent of the energy of most tsunamis by friction along the wave base. Areas that have narrow and steep continental shelves offshore are prone to the most severe tsunamis, since they do not have the ability to reduce the wave energy by friction.

Tsunami waves exhibit a phenomenon called *diffraction* when they enter bays through a narrow entrance. Diffraction occurs when energy moves or is leaked sideways along a wave crest, enabling the wave to grow along the wave front to fill the available area inside a wide bay that the wave has entered through a narrow opening. The wave front must enter through the narrow passage to the ocean, but then spreads across the bay as a longer wave. The process of *dispersion* moves energy from the initially high wave crest sideways and in doing so takes energy away from the central area, decreasing the height of the wave. Thus, energy dispersion during the wave's entrance and spread into the harbor is a good thing, reducing the threat to areas inside bays with narrow entrances. An example of a bay with a shape that would disperse tsunami energy is San Francisco Bay. If a tsunami were to pass under the Golden Gate Bridge it would crash through the narrows there, but then spread, losing height and ferocity, as it moved into the Bay Area.

The opposite effect of dispersion, *amplification,* occurs in bays where the opening of the bay or estuary is wide and the bay narrows

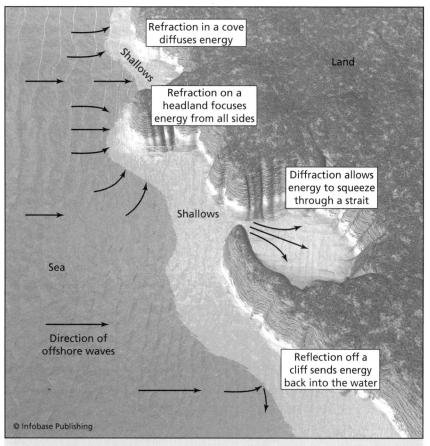

Refraction in a cove
diffuses energy

Shallows

Land

Refraction on a
headland focuses
energy from all sides

Diffraction allows
energy to squeeze
through a strait

Shallows

Sea

Direction of
offshore waves

Reflection off a
cliff sends energy
back into the water

© Infobase Publishing

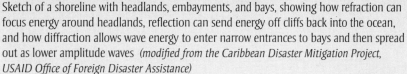

Sketch of a shoreline with headlands, embayments, and bays, showing how refraction can focus energy around headlands, reflection can send energy off cliffs back into the ocean, and how diffraction allows wave energy to enter narrow entrances to bays and then spread out as lower amplitude waves *(modified from the Caribbean Disaster Mitigation Project, USAID Office of Foreign Disaster Assistance)*

progressively inland. Tsunamis that enter such treacherous waters will find their wave crests being amplified or increased in height, transferring energy along the wave crest as they are forced to become shorter lengthwise. There are many examples of tsunami disasters that occurred because the shape of the bay amplified the tsunami that would otherwise have been minor. A famous example is the 1964 tsunami that hit Crescent City, California, induced from the magnitude 9.2 earthquake in Alaska. Most areas along the California coast experienced a relatively minor tsunami (less than 2 feet [0.5 m] in height), but the shape of the bay and seafloor at Crescent City amplified the wave until it consisted of a series of five tsunami crests. The fifth was a 21-foot- (6.4-m-) high crest that swept into downtown, washing away much of the waterfront district and killing 11 people.

When tsunamis strike the coastal environment, the first effect is sometimes a significant retreat or *drawdown* of the water level, whereas in other cases the water just starts to rise quickly. Since tsunamis have long wavelengths, it typically takes several minutes for the water to rise to its full height. Also, since there is no trough right behind the crest of the wave because of their very long wavelengths, the water does not recede for a considerable time after the initial crest rises onto land. The rate of rise of the water in a tsunami depends in part on the shape of the seafloor and coastline. If the seafloor rises slowly, the tsunami may crest slowly, giving people time to outrun the rising water. In other cases, especially where the seafloor rises steeply or the shape of the bay causes the wave to be amplified, tsunamis may come crashing in as huge walls of water with breaking waves that pummel the coast with a thundering roar, wreaking utmost destruction.

Because tsunamis are waves, they travel in successive crests and troughs. Many deaths in tsunamis are related to people going to the shoreline to investigate the effects of the first wave or to rescue those injured or killed in the initial crest, only to be drowned or swept away in a succeeding crest. Tsunamis have long wavelengths, so there is a long lag time between individual crests. The wave period can be an hour or more. Thus, a tsunami may devastate a shoreline area, retreat, and then another crest may strike an hour later, then another, and another in sequence.

The specific shape of any shoreline has large effects on the tsunami's height and the way it approaches the shoreline. The study of the effects of local coastal features on tsunamis is called *morphodynamics.* As the water from one wave crest retreats, it must move back to sea and interact with the next incoming wave. Some of this water moves quickly sideways along the coast, setting up a new independent set of waves that oscillates up and down in amplitude along the coast, typically with a wavelength that is double that of the original tsunami. These secondary waves are called *edge waves* and may be nearly as large as the original tsunami. When the following tsunami crests approach the shoreline, they may interact with a positive crest and produce a wave that is larger than the initial tsunami, or they may interact with a negative trough and produce a smaller wave. These edge waves and local morphodynamics explain much of the variability in the height of tsunamis along shorelines. In some locations, the tsunami crest may be 30 feet (10 m), while in nearby areas it may only be 6 feet (2 m).

The name *tsunami* means "harbor wave" in Japanese and describes another physical phenomena of waves called resonance. When waves enter harbors or bays, they have a characteristic period that in many cases matches a natural harmonic frequency of that particular harbor. This means that many tsunamis enter a bay and bounce back and forth across the harbor with the exact period that causes the wave to dramatically increase in height. The effect is similar to slowly moving a glass of water back and forth and gradually increasing the speed until suddenly the waves in the glass start to become amplified and leap out of the glass. This happens when the period of the wave equals that of the natural frequency of the glass. Many tsunamis that enter bays will *resonate,* or oscillate back and forth, in the bay for 24 hours or more, causing disruption of activities for an extended period.

## Tsunami Run-Up

*Run-up* is the height of the tsunami above sea level at the farthest point it reaches on the shore. This height may be considerably different from the height of the wave where it first hits the shore and is commonly twice that of the height of the wave at the shore. Run-up heights of 30 feet (10 m) are fairly common for tsunami, while heights of 150–300 feet (45–90 m) are rare, and heights greater than this in the range of 300–1,700 feet

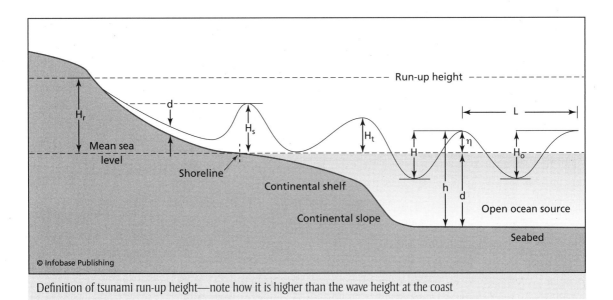

Definition of tsunami run-up height—note how it is higher than the wave height at the coast

(90–525 m) are very rare, but have been observed in the past 100 years. Many things influence the run-up of a tsunami, including the size of the wave, the shape of the shoreline, the profile of the water depth, diffraction, formation of edge waves that move along the coast, and other irregularities particular to individual areas. Some bays and other places along shorelines may amplify the effects of waves that come in from a certain direction, making run-ups higher than average. These areas are called *wave traps,* and in many cases the incoming waves form a moving crest of breaking water, called a *bore,* that smashes into coastal areas with great force. Tsunami magnitudes are commonly reported using the maximum run-up height along a particular coastline.

When tsunamis approach shore, the wave fronts pile up and the wave changes form from a sinusoidal wave to a solitary wave, with the entire wave form above sea level. These types of waves maintain their forms, and since the kinetic energy in the wave is evenly distributed throughout the wave, the waves lose very little energy as they approach the shore. Steep coastlines may experience larger run-ups since they have the least amount of energy dissipation. The shape and angles of cliffs along the beach can also in some cases amplify tsunami heights, in some cases tripling the height of the wave at the shore. Embayments that become narrower inland may amplify waves, and in some bays it may take two or even several tsunami crests for the amplification process to reach a maximum. Refraction effects can increase tsunami run ups around promontories.

In some cases, tsunamis are refracted around the shores of islands or both sides of bays, producing large edge waves that move parallel to shore. These edge waves must merge on the back sides of islands or in the ends of embayments, and in these locations particularly large run-ups have been recorded. Movement of edge waves around islands accounts for many of the large run-ups on the leeward sides of the Hawaiian Islands from the April 1, 1946, Hilo, Hawaii, tsunami, where many bays on the back sides of the islands experienced run-ups almost as high as those facing the initial wave front. The 1992 Flores Island tsunami also saw many villages on the leeward sides (facing away from the wave front) of islands washed away by large tsunamis. These waves were also formed by the waves being refracted around the islands, forming edge waves that combined to cause unusually large run-ups in specific locations. More than 2,000 people died when the 16–23 foot (5–7 m) waves washed into these villages on the back sides of the islands. Similarly, in a 1993 tsunami in Japan, the island of Okusihir focused the energy of a tsunami on the town of Hamat-sumae lying behind the island. On July 12, a 100-foot (30-m) wave grew behind the island and washed into the town, killing 330 people.

## Force of Tsunami Impact and Backwash

When tsunamis crash into coastal areas they are typically moving at about 22 MPH (35 km/hr). The speed as the wave moves inland changes dramatically, decreasing to a few MPH over short distances, depending on the slope of the beach or shore environment and how much resistance the wave encounters from obstacles on shore. The force associated with a debris-laden wall of water 50–70 miles (80–120 km) wide moving inland at that speed is tremendous. As tsunamis hit the shoreline and move inland they rapidly pick up debris and move this with the wave front, and these objects smash into whatever is in the path, destroying almost anything in the way. The force of the tsunami can be appreciated by considering the impact of a series of rocks thrown from a moving car or a train hitting a building at 22 MPH (35 km/hr). After the first impact the force of the wave does not stop but keeps on pounding

Photo of objects broken by force of wave—plank was forced through the tire during 1964 earthquake-related tsunami in Alaska *(USGS)*

into the coast until the crest passes, then the water continues to move inland and remain high for 30, 40, 50 minutes or more before retreating back to sea.

The force of the tsunami backwash can be just as strong and in some cases stronger than the initial impact. Some waves take five minutes or more to move inland and less than two minutes to wash back out to sea, so the outgoing velocity may be greater than the initial surge. The outgoing waves often take the loose debris from the destruction of the incoming wave with them, placing projectiles in the water for the next crest to launch when it moves inland.

Many tsunamis have been observed to form a thin wedge of turbulent water that shoots out in front of the wave crest with tremendous

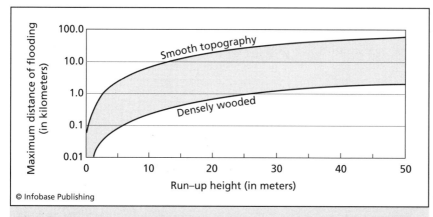

Chart showing tsunami run-up height versus the maximum landward distance of flooding. The diagram shows that areas with smooth topography flood much more than areas that are densely wooded. Cutting down coastal forests therefore increases the flooding and damage from tsunamis.

speed and force. These turbulent wedges of foamy debris-laden water do a lot of damage to buildings and vegetation just before the wave crest hits and may be associated with much higher velocities of projectiles than found in the main wave. These wedges may form by the weight of the wave compres sing air trapped in front of the wave and shooting this air-water-debris mixture out as the wave moves inland.

In many cases, the area of land that is flooded by a tsunami is roughly equal to the area found beneath the wave crest when it is close to shore. Larger tsunamis flood larger areas. The amount of flooding is greatest for flat open areas such as mudflats, pastures, etc., where the wave can move uninterruptedly inland. The amount of inland penetration decreases for areas that have forests, buildings, or other obstacles that slow the wave down. A moderate tsunami, about 30 feet (10 m) high, might penetrate a little less than a mile (1.6 km) inland in flat but developed coastal areas, half a mile (less than a km) in a developed downtown city environment, and perhaps 4 miles (6 km) on an undeveloped open coast. Dense coastal forests are able to significantly decrease the amount of inland penetration, taking much of the energy of the wave away as it must snap and move the trees to move further inland. Large tsunamis, greater than 160 feet (49 m) tall, can move inland 5–7 miles (9–12 km), while great tsunamis can theoretically reach tens of miles inland.

## Conclusion

Tsunamis generally present very minor hazards to those at sea, because of the low amplitude of the waves in deep ocean water. Exceptions may occur when the traveler is located very near the source of the tsunami. If an earthquake-induced tsunami occurs in shallow water, the initial wave close to the epicenter and displaced seafloor may be quite large, before it stabilizes into an organized, deepwater wave. If the tsunami is generated by a volcanic eruption, then the waves near the explosion may also be quite severe. Striking accounts of devastating near-source hazards of tsunami at sea are found in historical records of the 1883 eruption of Krakatau. Sea captains reported many vessels that were run aground or tipped by tsunamis in the Strait of Sunda near the eruption, and the waters were reportedly exceedingly rough and littered with pumice, corpses, and rubble for some time after the eruption.

The most serious tsunami hazards are associated with where the tsunami encounters shallow water and runs up onto land. In these coastal areas, the main hazard is from the wave itself, which can overtake and drown people and animals and destroy most structures in its path. Tsunamis also carry large amounts of debris that act as projectiles and can do serious damage when they crash into structures. Tsunamis also are known to have ruptured fuel storage tanks, started electrical fires, and eroded foundations, seawalls, and other constructions during their retreat from the land.

# 3

# Waves Similar to Tsunamis

Occasionally large waves, often solitary, wash up on otherwise placid coastal areas, overturning small craft and swamping beach areas. This chapter examines the processes in the ocean that can produce unusually large waves that may be mistaken as tsunamis. Some of these waves could be produced by amplification of passing ship wakes, while others seem to be meteorologically induced. The shape of some bays and estuaries amplifies waves that enter, which are characterized by large tidal bores and amplification of storm-related surges, and these too may be mistaken as tsunamis. Many coastlines are also occasionally influenced by storm surges, where water is pushed in front of powerful ocean storms as they move onto land.

## Seiche Waves and Meteorological Tsunamis

*Seiche waves* are similar to tsunamis, except that they are confined to enclosed bodies of water like lakes. They are generally generated by similar phenomena as tsunamis and may also be initiated by the rocking motion of the ground associated with large earthquakes. Many seiche waves were generated on lakes in southern Alaska during the 1964 magnitude 9.2 earthquake, including some on Kenai Lake that washed away piers and other structures near the shore. Seichelike waves sometimes resonate in bays and fjords during large earthquakes, but these are not truly seiche waves as they form in bodies of water connected to the sea.

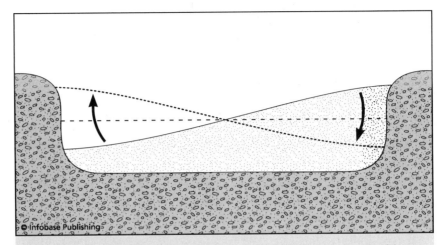

Sketch showing how a seiche wave oscillates in a lake. As the water on one side of the lake rises, it sinks on the opposite side. This process repeats, like a seesaw, sometimes for days after a significant disturbance such as an earthquake. (modified from Fisheries and Oceans Canada)

Certain types of meteorological phenomena can generate long-period waves with characteristics of tsunamis. These types of waves are well known in some regions and go by local names such as *abiki* or *yota* in Japan, *seebar* in the Baltic Sea, *marubbio* in Sicily, *rages* in the Bahamas, etc. They also occur in the eastern China seas, the Mediterranean, the Great Lakes of North America, and many other places worldwide. The southern end of Lake Michigan has experienced several significant meteorological tsunamis, with the largest one in recent history being a 10-foot (3-m) wave washing up near Chicago in 1954. Nagasaki Bay in Japan experiences a meteorological tsunami about once a year. On March 31, 1979, a particularly strong event produced a series of waves with heights between 9–16 feet (2.8–4.8 m) that oscillated back and forth in the bay every 35 minutes. The U.S. Marshall Islands in the western Pacific have experienced some very devastating waves that were probably of meteorological origin. On a clear, calm day in 1979, a 20-foot (6-m) wave suddenly rose from the ocean and passed over the protecting reefs around the islands, then crashed into the downtown business and residential areas of the town of Rita, destroying 144 homes. Another nearly identical wave struck the following day at high tide and then, a week after the first wave, a series of waves up to 27 feet (8 m) tall swept the islands, destroying homes, businesses, and the hospital. Damage was estimated at $20 million and the livelihoods of 8,000 people were affected.

Meteorological tsunamis tend to recur at specific locations and usually consist of a series of waves in a train. This makes them distinct from storm surges, consisting of a single wave. Each location is characterized by a specific period when these waves tend to oscillate, showing that they form through a combination of weather and pressure related effects and the shape of the lake that creates its own natural resonance, or wave period, that tends to be amplified by the weather conditions.

The atmospheric conditions that create meteorological tsunamis are associated with the passage of weather fronts, hurricanes or typhoons, large pressure jumps, and atmospheric gravity waves. Pressure differences on either side of a wide lake can cause the water to be pushed up from the high to the low pressure end of the atmospheric system. When this happens, the water may next collapse back and, if the shape of the lake is such that it amplifies this effect, the waves can grow in amplitude, producing significant seiche waves, or meteorological tsunamis.

## Tidal Surges

Tides are the periodic rise and fall of the ocean surface and alternate submersion and exposure of the intertidal zone along coasts. Along most coastlines, tides rise and fall slowly, but in some places and in rare situations, tides may rise suddenly and dramatically and mimic the effects of tsunamis. Currents caused by the rise and fall of the sea surface are the strongest currents in the ocean and were attributed to the gravitational effects of the Sun and Moon since at least the times of Pliny the Elder (23–79 c.e.).

The range in sea surface height between the high and low tides is known as the *tidal range,* and this varies considerably from barely detectable to more than 50 feet (15 m). Most places have two high tides and two low tides each tidal day, a period of about 24 hours and 50 minutes, corresponding to the time between successive passes of the Moon over any point. The tidal period is the time between successive high or low tides. Places with two high and two low tides per day have semidaily, or semidiurnal, tides. Fewer places have only one high and one low tide per day, a cycle referred to as a diurnal, or daily, tide. Semidiurnal tides are often not equal in heights between the two highs and two lows.

Spring tides are those that occur near the full and new Moons and have a tidal range larger than the mean tidal range. In contrast, neap tides occur during the first and third quarters of the Moon and are characterized by lower than average tidal ranges.

Sir Isaac Newton was the first to clearly elucidate the mechanics of tides and how they are related to the gravitational attraction of the Moon. In his equilibrium theory of tides, he assumed a nonrotating Earth, covered with water and having no continents. In this simplified model aimed at understanding the origin of tides, gravitational attraction pulls the Earth and Moon toward each other, while centrifugal forces act in the opposite direction and keep them apart. Since the Moon is so much smaller than the Earth, the center of mass and rotation of the Earth-Moon system is located within the Earth 2,900 miles (4,670 km) from the Earth's center, on the side of the Earth closest to the Moon. This causes unbalanced forces since a unit of water on the Earth's surface closest to the Moon is located 59 Earth radii from the Moon's surface, whereas a unit of water on the opposite side of the Earth is located 61 Earth radii from the nearest point on the Moon. Since the force of gravity is inversely proportional to the distance squared between the two points, the Moon's gravitational pull is much greater for the unit of water closer to the Moon. However, centrifugal forces that act perpendicular to the axis of rotation of the Earth also affect the tides and must be added with the gravitational forces to yield a vector sum that is the tide-producing force. Together, these forces result in the gravitational

Photo of tidal bore moving up Turnagain Arm, a fjord that branches off Cook Inlet in southern Alaska. The tidal range here is up to 40 feet (13 m), aiding the formation of the bore. *(USGS)*

force of the Moon exceeding the centrifugal force on the side of Earth closest to the Moon, drawing water in a bulge toward the Moon. On the opposite side of the Earth the centrifugal force overbalances the gravitational attraction of the Moon so there the water is essentially dragged away from the Earth.

The interaction of the gravitational and centrifugal forces creates a more complex pattern of tides on Newton's model Earth. Directly beneath the Moon and on the opposite side of the Earth, both the gravitational force and the centrifugal force act perpendicular to the surface, but elsewhere the vector sum of the two forces is not perpendicular to the surface. The result of adding the centrifugal force and gravity vectors is a two-sided egg-shaped bulge that points toward and away from the Moon. Newton called these bulges the equilibrium tide. The situation is however even more complex, since the Sun also exerts a gravitational attraction on the Earth and its water, forming an additional egg-shaped bulge that is about 0.46 times as large as the lunar tidal bulge.

If one considers the Earth to be rotating through the tidal bulges on a water-covered planet, the simplest situation arises with two high tides and two low tides each day, since the lunar tides dominate over the effects of the solar tides. However, the Earth has continents that hinder the equal flow of water and bays and estuaries that trap and amplify the tides in certain places, plus frictional drag slows the passage of the tidal bulge through shallow waters. In addition, the *Coriolis effect* must be taken into account as tides involve considerable movement of water from one place to another. These obstacles cause the tides to be different at different places on the Earth, explaining the large range in observed tidal ranges and periods.

In some of the world's bays and estuaries the shape of the coastline tends to funnel water from the rising tides into narrower and narrower places, causing the water to pile up. When this happens, the volume of water entering the bay forms a wave called a tidal bore that moves inland, typically growing in height and forward velocity as the bay becomes narrower and narrower. Places with famous tidal bores and large tidal ranges include the Bay of Fundy in eastern Canada, Cook Inlet in Alaska, and parts of the North Sea in Europe. These tidal bores resemble tsunamis in that they are long-wavelength phenomena, rise into coastal areas at high velocities, and can be deadly to unsuspecting beachgoers. Tidal bores are regularly repeating phenomena, however, and shorelines that experience these have distinctive tide-eroded landscapes and residents have adapted their lifestyles according to the movements of the tides.

## Storm Surges

Some types of ocean storms such as hurricanes are associated with large, long-wavelength waves called storm surges that may mimic the effects of tsunamis. Hurricanes are intense tropical storms with sustained winds of more than 74 MPH (119 km/hr) that form in the northern Atlantic or eastern Pacific Oceans, known as cyclones if they form in the Indian Ocean of Australia and typhoons if they form in the western Pacific Ocean. Most large hurricanes have a central eye with calm or light winds and clear skies or broken clouds, surrounded by an eye wall, a ring of very tall and intense thunderstorms that spin around the eye, with some of the most intense winds and rain of the entire storm system. The eye is surrounded by spiral rain bands that spin counterclockwise in the Northern Hemisphere (clockwise in the Southern Hemisphere) in toward the eye wall, moving faster and generating huge waves as they approach the center. Wind speeds increase toward the center of the storm and the atmospheric pressure decreases to a low in the eye, uplifting the sea surface in the storm center. Surface air flows in toward the eye of the hurricane, then moves upward, often above nine miles (15 km), along the eye wall. From there it moves outward in a large outflow, until it descends outside the spiral rain bands. Air in the rain bands is ascending, whereas between the rain bands, belts of descending air counter this flow. Air in the very center of the eye descends to the surface. Hurricanes drop enormous amounts of precipitation, typically spawn numerous tornadoes, and cause intense coastal damage from winds, waves, and storm surges, where the sea surface may be elevated tens of feet above its normal level.

The greatest number of deaths from hurricanes has been from effects of the storm surge. Storm surges typically come ashore as a wall of water that rushes onto land at the forward velocity of the hurricane, as the storm waves on top of the surge are pounding the coastal area with additional energy. For instance, when Hurricane Camille hit Mississippi in 1969 with 200 MPH winds (322 km/hr), a 24-foot- (7.3-m-) high storm surge moved into coastal areas, killing most of the 256 people who perished in this storm.

Storm surges consist of water that is pushed ahead of storms and typically moves on land as exceptionally high tides in front of severe ocean storms such as hurricanes. Storms that produce surges include hurricanes (which form in the late summer and fall) and extratropical lows (which form in the late fall through spring). Hurricanes originate in the Tropics and (for North America) migrate westward and northwestward before turning back to the northeast to return to the cold North Atlantic, weakening the storm. North Atlantic hurricanes are driven to

Storm surges form from low pressure inside storms such as hurricanes lifting the sea surface and from masses of water pushed ashore in front of the moving storms. With large waves on top of elevated sea levels, storm surges can resemble tsunamis, except that storm surges come as single waves and may cause the water to remain high for many hours.

the west by the trade winds and bend to the right because the Coriolis force makes objects moving above Earth's surface appear to curve to the right in the Northern Hemisphere. Hurricane paths are further modified by other weather conditions, such as the location of high and low pressure systems, and their interaction with weather fronts. Extratropi-

## STORM SURGE FROM THE GALVESTON ISLAND HURRICANE, 1900

The deadliest natural disaster to affect the United States was when a category 4 hurricane with a huge storm surge hit Galveston Island, Texas, on September 8, 1900. Galveston is a low-lying *barrier island* located south of Houston and in 1900 was a wealthy port city. Residents of coastal Texas received early warning of an approaching hurricane from a Cuban meteorologist, but most chose to ignore this advice. Perhaps too late, U.S. forecasters warned of an approaching hurricane, and many people then evacuated the island to move to relative safety inland. However, many others remained on the island. In the late afternoon the hurricane moved in to Galveston, and a massive storm surge hit at high tide covering the entire island with water. Even the highest point on the island was covered with one foot (0.3 m) of water. Winds of 120 MPH (190 km/hr) destroyed wooden buildings, as well as many of the stronger brick structures. Debris from destroyed buildings crashed into standing structures, demolishing them and creating a moving mangled mess, trapping residents on the island. The storm continued through the night, battering the island and city with 30-foot- (9-m-) high waves, over the height of the storm surge. In the morning, residents who had found shelter emerged to see half of the city totally destroyed and the other half severely damaged. But worst of all, thousands of bodies were strewn everywhere, 6,000 on Galveston Island and another 1,500 on the mainland. There was no way off the island as all boats and bridges were destroyed, so survivors were in additional danger of disease from the decaying bodies. When help arrived from the mainland, the survivors needed to dispose of the bodies before cholera set in, so they put the decaying corpses on barges and dumped them at sea. However, the tides and waves soon brought the bodies back and they eventually had to be burned in giant funeral pyres built with wood from the destroyed city. Galveston was rebuilt and a seawall built from stones was supposed to protect the city; however, in 1915, another hurricane struck Galveston, claiming 275 additional lives.

The Galveston seawall has since been reconstructed and is higher and stronger, although some forecasters believe that even this seawall will not be able to protect the city from a category 5 hurricane. Additionally, the land surface on Galveston Island is sinking at up to one inch (2.5 cm) per year, and as sea levels rise and the land sinks Galveston will become more susceptible to hurricane storm surge damage. The possibility of a surprise storm hitting Galveston again is not so remote, as demonstrated by the surprise tropical storm of early June 2001. Weather forecasters were not successful in predicting the rapid strengthening and movement of this storm, which dumped 23–48 inches (58–122 cm) of rain on different parts of the Galveston-Houston area and attacked the seawall and coastal structures with huge waves and 30 MPH (48 km/hr) winds. Twenty-two people died in the area from the surprise storm, showing that even modern weather forecasting cannot always adequately predict tropical storms. It is best to heed early warnings and prepare for rapidly changing conditions when hurricanes and tropical storms are approaching vulnerable areas.

cal lows (also known as coastal storms, and nor'easters) move eastward across North America and typically intensify when they hit the Atlantic and move up the coast. Both types of storms rotate counterclockwise and the low pressure at the centers of the storms raises the water several to several tens of feet. This extra water moves ahead of the storms as a storm surge that represents an additional height of water above the normal tidal range. The wind from the storms adds further height to the storm surge, with the total height of the storm surge being determined by the length, duration, and direction of wind, plus how low the pressure gets in the center of the storm. The most destructive storm surges are those that strike low-lying communities at high tide, as the effects of the storm surge and the regular astronomical tides are cumulative. They are capable of removing entire beaches, rows of homes, causing great amounts of cliff erosion, and significantly redistributing sands in dunes and the back beach environment. Very precise prediction of the height and timing of the approach of the storm surge is necessary to warn coastal residents of when they need to evacuate and when it is not necessary to leave their homes.

As with many natural catastrophic events, the heights of storm surges are statistically predictable. If the height of storm surges is plotted on a semilogarithmic plot, with the height plotted in a linear interval and the frequency (in years) plotted on a logarithmic scale, then a linear slope results. This means that communities can plan for storm surges of certain heights to occur once every 50, 100, 300, or 500 years, although there is no way to predict when the actual storm surges will occur. It must be remembered that this is a long-term statistical average, and that one, two, three, or more 500-year events may occur over a relatively short period, but, averaged over a long time, the events average out to once every 500 years.

The strength of hurricanes is measured using the Saffir-Simpson scale, which measures the damage potential of a storm, considering such factors as the central barometric pressure, maximum sustained wind speeds, and the potential height of the storm surge. Category 1 hurricanes have central pressures of greater than 980 millibars, sustained winds 74–95 MPH (119–153 km/hr), and a likely 4–5 foot (1–1.5 m) storm surge. Damage potential is minimal, with likely effects including downed power lines, ruined crops, and minor damage to weak parts of buildings. Category 2 hurricanes have central barometric pressures of 979–965 millibars, maximum sustained winds of 96–110 MPH (155–177 km/hr), and 6–8 foot (1.8–2.4 m) storm surges. Damage is typically moderate, including roof and chimney damage, beached and splintered boats, destroyed crops, road signs, and traffic lights. Category 3 hurricanes have central barometric pressures of 964–945 millibars, sustained winds of 111–130 MPH (179–209 km/hr), and storm surges of 9–12 feet (2.7–3.6 m). Category 3 hurricanes are major storms capable of extensive property damage including uprooting large trees and the destruction of mobile homes and poorly constructed coastal houses. Category 4 storms can be devastating, with central barometric pressures of 940–920 millibars, sustained winds of 131–155 MPH (211–249 km/hr), and storm surges of 13–18 feet (4–5.5 m). These storms typically rip the roofs off homes, businesses, destroy sea piers, and throw boats well inland. Waves may breach seawalls causing large-scale coastal flooding. Category 5 storms are truly massive, with central barometric pressures dropping below 920 millibars, maximum sustained winds above 155 MPH (249 km/hr), and storm surges over 18 feet (5.5 m). Storms with this power rarely hit land but when they do they are capable of leveling entire towns, moving large amounts of coastal sediments, and causing large death tolls.

Storm surges are similar to tsunamis in some ways, but storm surges are single waves, in contrast to tsunamis that travel in wave trains. For instance, the 1938 Long Island hurricane had a single, 43-foot- (13-m-) tall wall of water move onshore, causing great damage. Hurricane Katrina in 2005 was associated with large storm surges along the Gulf of Mexico and in New Orleans, where sea levels rose by up to tens of feet and stayed high for hours as the storm pounded the shoreline environment. Storm surges thus are quite different from tsunamis that travel in wave trains, typically rising and retreating in cycles of under an hour per wave front.

## Conclusion

Several processes produce long-period waves that mimic the effects of tsunamis. Meteorological tsunamis or seiches are produced when there are large pressure differences on either side of large lakes and water is pushed higher on one side than the other. In some cases, the natural resonance of the lake serves to amplify this effect, setting up an oscillation where the waves move back and forth, typically with a period of more than half an hour, for a day or more.

Tidal surges are produced in places where the shape of the coastline amplifies the effect of the incoming tide, forcing more water into confined passages, and forming a wave known as a tidal bore. These move inland, but are regular predictable events that occur with the repetition of the tide.

Storm surges are masses of water pushed in front of powerful storms such as hurricanes and move ashore as solitary waves that may raise sea levels by tens of feet, with large waves from the storm crashing in on top of the elevated sea level. Storm surges differ from tsunamis not only in their origins, but also in that they are solitary waves, and tsunamis strike as a series of waves in a wave train. Both can be deadly for people on the coast and cause catastrophic damage to shoreline communities.

# 4

# Historical Tsunami Disasters

Tsunamis have taken hundreds of thousands of lives in the past few hundred years, and some of the larger tsunamis have caused millions to billions of dollars in damage. This chapter examines some of the most significant events of the past few hundred years, looking at the causes, consequences, and what has been learned from each example. The tsunami disasters are discussed according to their triggering mechanisms. The table on the following page lists significant tsunamis that are well documented in recorded history and helps put the historical tsunamis discussed in the chapter in perspective.

## Earthquake-Induced Tsunamis

### EASTERN ATLANTIC TSUNAMI, NOVEMBER 1, 1755

Tsunamis do not regularly strike Atlantic regions, with only about 10 percent of all tsunamis occurring in the Atlantic Ocean. A few have been associated with earthquakes in the Caribbean region, such as in 1867 in the Virgin Islands, in 1918 in Puerto Rico, and on June 6, 1692, when 3,000 people were killed by a tsunami that leveled Port Royal, Jamaica. The most destructive tsunami in history to hit the Atlantic region struck on November 1, 1755. Lisbon, Portugal, was the worst hit because it was near the epicenter of the earthquake that initiated the tsunami. At least three large waves, each 15–40 feet (4–12 m) high, struck Lisbon in quick succession, killing at least 60,000 people in Lisbon alone. England was hit by 6–10 foot (2–3 m) waves, and the tsunami even affected the

Caribbean region, hitting Antigua with 12–foot (3.6-m) waves and Saba and St. Martin with waves more than 15 feet (4.6 m) high.

The Lisbon-Eastern Atlantic tsunami was generated by a large earthquake whose epicenter was located about 60 miles (100 km) southwest of Lisbon, probably on the boundary of the European and Azores-Gibraltar plates. The earthquake had an estimated magnitude of 9.0 and the shaking lasted for 10 minutes. During this time, three exceptionally large jolts occurred, causing massive destruction in Lisbon and the Moroccan towns of Fez and Mequinez. Much of Europe including Scandinavia reported seiche waves on lakes and inland water bodies.

The earthquake caused extensive damage to the city of Lisbon, toppling many buildings and causing widespread and uncontrolled fires. In

| The Deadliest Tsunamis in History | | |
|---|---|---|
| LOCATION | YEAR | NUMBER OF DEATHS |
| Indian Ocean | 2004 | > 283,000 dead across region |
| Santorini | c. 1550 B.C.E. | devastation of Mediterranean |
| Eastern Atlantic | Nov. 1, 1755 | 60,000 dead in Lisbon Est. 100,000 total |
| Messina, Italy | 1908 | 70,000 dead |
| Taiwan | May 22, 1782 | 50,000 dead |
| Nainkaido, Japan | Oct. 28, 1707 | 30,000 dead |
| Krakatau, Indonesia | Aug. 27, 1883 | 36,500 dead |
| Sanriku, Japan | June 15, 1896 | 27,122 dead |
| Nainkaido, Japan | Sept. 20, 1498 | 26,000 dead |
| Arica, Chile | Aug. 13, 1868 | 25,674 dead |
| Sagamai Bay, Japan | May 27, 1293 | 23,024 dead |
| Guatemala | Feb. 4, 1976 | 22,778 dead |
| Lima, Peru | Oct. 29, 1746 | 18,000 dead |
| Bali, Indonesia | Jan. 21, 1917 | 15,000 dead |

| LOCATION | YEAR | NUMBER OF DEATHS |
|---|---|---|
| Unzen, Japan | May 21, 1792 | 14,524 dead |
| Ryuku, Japan | April 24, 1771 | 13,486 dead |
| Bali, Indonesia | Nov. 22, 1815 | 10,253 dead |
| Guanzhou, China | May 1765 | 10,000 dead |
| Moro Bay, Philippines | Aug. 16, 1976 | 8,000 dead |
| Honshu, Japan | March 2, 1933 | 3,000 dead |
| Indonesia | Dec. 12, 1992 | 2,000 dead |
| Chile | May 22, 1960 | 2,231 known dead/missing, Est. 10,000 dead |
| Aleutians | April 1, 1946 | 150 in Hawaii, 25 million dollars in damage |
| Alaska | March 28, 1964 | 119 dead in California, $104 million in damage |
| Nicaragua | Sept. 2, 1992 | 170 dead |
| Indonesia | Dec. 2, 1992 | 137 dead |

fear, many residents ran to the city docks in the harbor and on the Tagus River. As the buildings continued to collapse and the fire raged through the city, driving much of the population of 275,000 people to the waterfront, the worst part of this disaster was about to unfold. About 40 to 60 minutes after the massive earthquake, residents of Lisbon watched from the docks as the water rapidly drained out of the harbor, as if someone had pulled the plug in the bottom of a bathtub. A few minutes later, a massive wall of water 50 feet (15 m) high swept up the harbor and over the docks and then more than 10 miles (16 km) upriver. It was followed by a powerful backwash that dragged tens of thousands of people and debris into the harbor. Two more giant waves rushed into the city an hour apart and killed more of the terrified residents trapped between raging tsunami waves and a city crumbling under the forces of fire and earthquake aftershocks. About 60,000 people, nearly one-quarter of the city's population, perished in the tsunami.

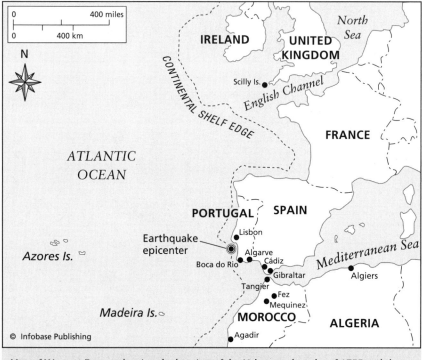

Map of Western Europe showing the location of the Lisbon earthquake of 1755 and the areas strongly affected by the associated tsunami

The November 1, 1755, earthquake caused extensive damage across the eastern Atlantic Ocean, with tsunamis sweeping the coasts of North Africa, Portugal, Spain, France, and the British Isles. Even islands in the Caribbean were affected. The tsunami moved inland 1.5 miles (2.5 km) across low-lying areas of Portugal, and run-up heights around Portugal reached 65–100 feet (20–35 m) above sea level. Southern Portugal was the worst hit, with medieval fortresses and towns destroyed or suffering heavy damage. The tsunami washed over the ancient walled city of Lagos, whose walls are anchored 36 feet (11 m) above sea level. The walls reduced the force of the waves, but the city was flooded and the water had to drain out of the narrow city gates, dragging many of the contents of the city to sea. The initial wave was followed by at least 18 secondary crests in southern Portugal, each adding damage to the effects of the previous wave.

Western Europe was strongly hit as the tsunami spread northward. The south coast of England saw massive waves that tore up the coastal muds and sandbars and swept into the shores of the Bay of Biscay. Boats in the North Sea were ripped from their moorings. The English Channel

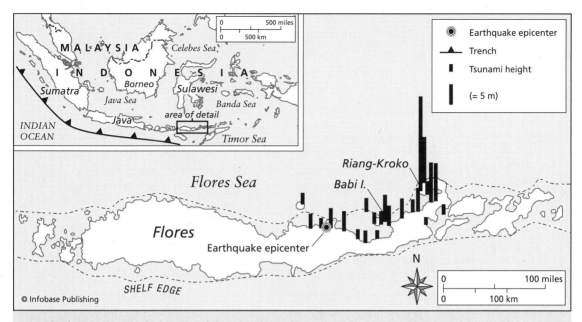

Map of Indonesia showing the location of Flores, on the back-arc side of the island, which was hit by a strong tsunami on December 12, 1992

was swept by waves 10–13 feet (3–4 m) high at high tide, followed by even higher waves that oscillated every 10 to 20 minutes over the next five hours. The Azores, located off the coast of Portugal, were hit by 50-foot (15-m) waves as they raced across the Atlantic to the eastern seaboard of North America. Caribbean islands were hit by tsunamis with run-up heights in the range of 20–25 feet (6–7.6 m), with the worst-hit areas reported to be Saint Martin and Saba. Elsewhere in the Caribbean, 10–15 foot (3–4.6 m) waves were reported to have oscillated every five minutes for about three hours, affecting many harbor and coastal areas.

## THE FLORES, INDONESIA, TSUNAMI, DECEMBER 12, 1992

One of the more deadly tsunamis in recent history hit the island of Flores, located in Indonesia several hundred miles from the coast of northern Australia near the popular resort island of Bali. The tsunami hit on December 12, 1992, triggered by a magnitude 7.9 earthquake, with the earthquake faulting event lasting for a long 70 seconds. The tsunami had run-up heights of 15–90 feet (4–27 m) along the northeastern part of Flores Island, where more than 2,080 people were killed and at least another 2,000 injured. It is believed that large amounts of sediment slumped underwater on the north side of the island during the earthquake, generating the unusually large and destructive tsunami.

Flores is an island located above the subduction zone where the Indian-Australian plate is being pushed beneath the Eurasian plate, along a convergent boundary. This subduction zone produces some of the largest earthquakes and tsunamis in the world, including the massive December 24, 2004, Indian Ocean tsunami. The earthquake that generated the Flores tsunami had its epicenter near the coast and produced *subsidence* of 1.5–3.5 feet (0.5–1.1 m). Unlike most other tsunami-generating earthquakes in this part of the world, this earthquake was located on the back-arc side of the island, away from the trench and forearc. The type of fault that forms on the back-arc is called a back-thrust, which is what slipped, producing the Flores tsunami.

There was very little warning for the residents of Flores Island, because the epicenter of the earthquake that generated the tsunami was only 30 miles (50 km) off the northern coast of the island. The first waves hit less than five minutes after the initial earthquake shock, with five or six individual waves being recorded by residents in different places. Many places recorded three large waves, the first one preceded by a rapid withdrawal of water from the coast, then the wave arrived as a wall of water. In most locations the second wave was the largest, with run-up heights typically between 6–16 feet (2–5 m). However, run-up heights in the village of Riang-Kroko were amplified to an astounding 86 feet (26.2 m), explaining why 137 of the 406 residents of the village were killed. Another hard-hit area was Babi Island, located three miles (5 km) offshore from Flores. The tsunami approached the island from the northeast and refracted around the island, until the edge waves met on the southwest corner and combined to produce a larger wave with run-up heights of 24 feet (7.2 m). The first, direct wave from the tsunami had a run-up velocity of 3.2 feet per second (1 m/sec), whereas the wave produced by the combined edge waves had a faster run-up velocity of up to 10 feet per second (3 m/sec). The island had 1,093 inhabitants, and 263 were washed away and drowned by the tsunami.

The residents of Flores were unaware that they lived in a tsunami hazard area, and they did not connect the ground shaking with possible sea hazards. Therefore, no warnings were issued and nobody fled the coastal areas after the quake. The villagers had built their homes and villages right along the coastline not far above the high-tide line, further compounding the threat. Many of the homes were made of bricks, but even these relatively strong structures were washed away by the tsunami. In some cases, the concrete foundations of the basement moved many tens of feet inland as coherent blocks as the tsunami

Debris and tuna line the streets of Flores Island after the 1992 tsunami. *(Reuters/CORBIS)*

rushed across the area, with its associated strong currents. In this way, the tsunami made a less-than-subtle suggestion about where the safe building zone should begin. When the tsunami receded, 2,080 people were dead, 28,118 homes were washed away, and thousands of other structures were leveled. In many cases only white wave-washed beaches remained where once there were villages with populations of hundreds of people. Houses, furniture, clothing, animals, and human remains were scattered through the forests behind the villages.

The Flores tsunami also caused severe coastal erosion, including cliff collapse and the scouring of coral reef complexes. Forests, brush, and grasses were removed, leaving vegetated hilltops and barren areas along the lower slopes of the coastal hills. Thick deposits of loose sediment were moved inland and also were redeposited as sheets of sediment in deeper water by the tsunami backwash, causing a sudden erosion of the land. Some large coral reef boulders, up to four feet (1 m) in diameter, were moved inland many hundreds of feet (100 m) from the shoreline.

## NICARAGUA TSUNAMI, SEPTEMBER 1, 1992

The west coast of Nicaragua and Central America is on a convergent margin where the oceanic crust of the Cocos plate (a small plate attached to the Pacific Ocean plate) is being subducted beneath the western edge

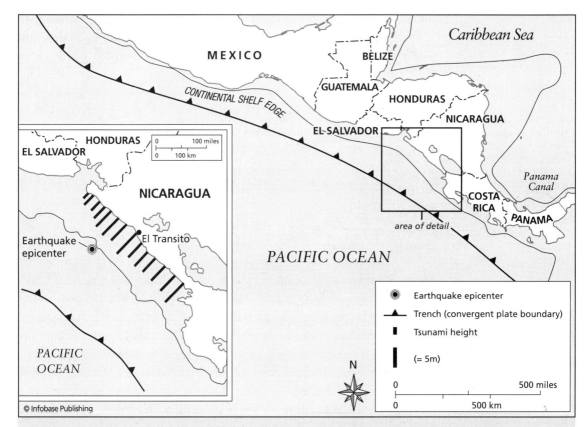

Map of Nicaragua showing convergent plate boundary (trench) and height of the September 2, 1992, tsunami

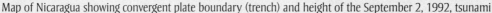

of the Caribbean plate. A volcanic arc with active volcanoes, earthquakes, and steep mountains has formed above this convergent margin subduction zone. The area is prone to large earthquakes in the forearc, to explosive volcanic eruptions, and also suffers from many hurricanes, landslides, and other natural disasters.

On September 1, 1992, a relatively small (magnitude 7) earthquake centered 30 miles (50 km) off the coast of Managua, Nicaragua, generated a huge tsunami that swept across 200 miles (320 km) of coastline, killing 170 people and making 14,500 more homeless. This tsunami was generated by a tsunamogenic earthquake that ruptured near the surface, with a shallow focus of only 28 miles (45 km). The earthquake struck in an area where thick sediments have been subducted and are now plastered along the interface between the downgoing oceanic plate and the overriding continental plate of Central America. It has been suggested that these sediments lubricated the fault plane and caused the earthquake to rupture slowly and last a particularly long time, generating an unusually large tsunami for an earthquake of this size. After the fault plane initially slipped at depth, the rupture propagated outward and to the surface at a speed of 0.5–1 mile per second (1–1.5 km/sec), with the movement lasting for two minutes. The slow speed of the movement of the ground in this earthquake made the motion barely perceptible to people on the surface, but was at the perfect speed for effectively moving large volumes of water as the seafloor was displaced. Slow earthquakes like this one are now known to be particularly dangerous for generating tsunamis and are known as tsunamogenic earthquakes. The height of the Nicaraguan tsunami was about 10 times greater than predicted for an earthquake of this magnitude.

The tsunami that was generated by the slow Nicaraguan earthquake of 1992 was up to 40 feet (12 m) high at nearby beachfronts, and it swept homes, vehicles, and unsuspecting people to sea within 40 minutes of the earthquake. The tsunami had a relatively slow run-up velocity, so that many people were able to outrun the wave, but elderly, sick, sleeping, and sedentary people and young children could not escape. The beachfront was heavily damaged, and 170 people were drowned by the tsunami. After the initial disaster, the hazards were not over, because the tsunami had ripped through water storage and sewage treatment plants, and the resulting contamination caused an outbreak of cholera that took even more lives in the following weeks.

## ALASKA EARTHQUAKE-RELATED TSUNAMI, MARCH 27, 1964

Southern Alaska is hit by a significant tsunami every 10 to 30 years. The earthquakes are generated along the convergent plate boundary where oceanic crust of the Pacific plate is being pushed back into the mantle beneath Alaska. The continental crust of the North American plate in Alaska is moving over the Pacific plate, along a huge fault zone known as the Aleutian-Alaska megathrust zone, which is part of the subduction zone between the Pacific and North American plates. This fault dips at only 20 degrees north, so motion on the fault causes large displacements of the seafloor and hence generates large tsunamis. This fault zone has generated large Pacific Ocean tsunamis in 1878, 1946, 1957, and 1964, with many smaller events in between. During the magnitude 9.2 March 27, 1964, earthquake in Alaska, approximately 35,000 square miles (90,650 sq km) of seafloor and adjacent land were suddenly thrust upward by up to 65 feet (20 m), as part of more regional movements of the land during this event. It is estimated that displacement of about 83,000 square miles (215,000 sq km) of seafloor moved significantly upward, while other areas of southern Alaska moved downward. This mass movement generated a huge tsunami, as well as many related seichelike waves in surrounding bays. The tsunami generated from this earthquake caused widespread destruction in Alaska, especially in Seward, Valdez, and Whittier. These towns all experienced large earthquake-induced submarine landslides, some of which tore away parts of the towns' waterfronts. The submarine landslides also generated large tsunamis that cascaded over these towns barely after the ground stopped shaking from the earthquake.

The "Good Friday" earthquake that struck southern Alaska at 5:36 P.M. on Friday, March 27, 1964, was one of the largest earthquakes ever recorded, second in the amount of energy released only to the 1960 Chile earthquake and followed closely by the 2004 Sumatra magnitude 9.0 earthquake. The epicenter was located in northern Prince William Sound, and the focus, or point of initial rupture, was located at a remarkably shallow 14 miles (23 km) beneath the surface. The energy released during the Valdez earthquake was more than the world's largest nuclear explosion and greater than the Earth's total average annual release of seismic energy, yet, remarkably, only 131 people died during this event. Damage is estimated at $240 million (1964 dollars), a surprisingly small figure for an earthquake this size. During the initial shock and several other shocks that followed in the next one to two minutes, a 600-mile- (1,000-km-) long by 250-mile- (400-km-) wide slab of subducting oceanic crust slipped further beneath the North American crust of southern Alaska. Ground displacements above the area that slipped were tremendous—much of the Prince William Sound and Kenai Peninsula area moved horizontally almost 65 feet (20 m) and moved upward by more than 35 feet (10.7 m). Other areas more landward of the uplifted zone were down dropped by several to 10 feet. Overall, almost 200,000 square miles (520,000 sq km) of land saw significant movement upward, downward, and laterally during this huge earthquake. These movements suddenly displaced an estimated volume of water of 6,000 cubic miles (25,000 cubic km).

The ground shook in most places for three to four minutes during the March 27, 1964, earthquake, but lasted for as much as seven minutes in a few places such as Anchorage and Valdez where unconsolidated sediment and fill amplified and prolonged the shaking. The shaking caused widespread destruction in southern Alaska, damage as far away as southern California, and induced noticeable effects across the planet. Entire neighborhoods and towns slipped into the sea during this earthquake, and ground breaks, landslides, and slumps were reported across the entire region. The Hanning Bay Fault on Montague Island, near the epicenter, broke through the surface, forming a spectacular fault scarp with a displacement of more than 15 feet (4.6 m), uplifting beach terraces and mussel beds above the high-water mark, many parts of which rapidly eroded to a more stable configuration. Urban areas such as Anchorage suffered numerous landslides and slumps, with tremendous damage done by translational slumps where huge blocks of soils and rocks slid downslope on curved faults, in many cases toward the sea. Houses ended up in neighbors' backyards, and some homes were split in two by ground breaks. A neighborhood in Anchorage known as Turnagain Heights suffered extensive damage when huge sections of the underlying ground slid toward the sea on a weak layer in the bedrock known as the Bootlegger Shale, which lost cohesion during the earthquake's shaking.

The transportation system in Alaska was severely disrupted by the earthquake. All major highways and most secondary roads suffered damage to varying degrees—186 of 830 miles (300 of 1,340 km) of roads were damaged, and 83 miles (125 km) of roadway needed replacement. Seventy-five percent of all bridges collapsed, became unusable, or suffered severe damage. Many railroad tracks were severed or bent by movement on faults, sliding and slumping into streams, and other ground motions. In Seward, Valdez, Kodiak, and other coastal communities, a series of 3–10 tsunami waves tore trains from their tracks, throwing them explosively onto higher ground. The shipping industry was devastated, which was especially difficult as Alaskans used shipping for more than 90 percent of their transportation needs, and the main industry in the state is fishing. All port facilities in southern Alaska except those in Anchorage were totally destroyed by submarine slides, tsunamis, tectonic uplift and subsidence, and earthquake-induced fires. Huge portions of the waterfront facilities at Seward and Valdez slid under the sea during a series of submarine landslides, resulting in the loss of the harbor facilities and necessitating the eventual moving of the cities to higher, more stable ground. Being thrown to higher ground destroyed hundreds of boats, although no large vessels were lost. Uplift in many shipping channels formed new hazards and obstacles that had to be mapped to avoid grounding and puncturing hulls. Downed lines disrupted communication systems, and initial communications with remote communities were taken over by small, independently powered radio operators. Water, sewer, and petroleum storage tanks

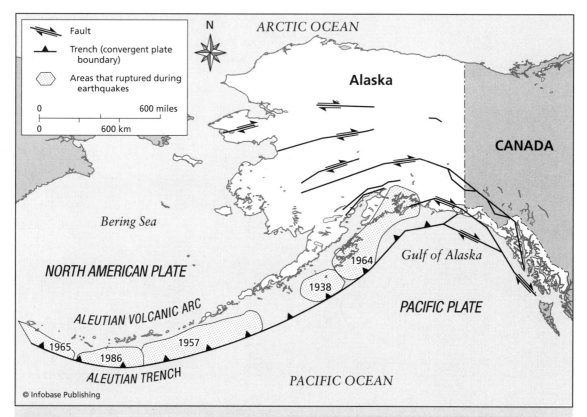

Map of fault rupture areas showing large historical earthquakes related to subduction of the Pacific plate beneath the North American plate, forming the Aleutian volcanic arc

and gas lines were broken, exploded, and generally disrupted by slumping, landslides, and ground movements. Residents were forced to obtain water and fuel that was trucked into areas for many months while supply lines were restored. Groundwater levels generally dropped, in some cases below well levels, further compounding the problems of access to freshwater.

Most damage from the 1964 Alaskan earthquake was associated with the numerous tsunamis and seiche waves generated during this event. A major Pacific-wide tsunami was generated by the large movements of the seafloor and continental shelf, whereas other tsunamis were generated by displacements of the seafloor near Montague Island in Prince William Sound, by landslides, and by natural resonance in the many bays and fjords of southern Alaska.

The town of Seward on the Kenai Peninsula experienced strong ground shaking for about four minutes during the earthquake, and this initiated a series of particularly large submarine landslides and

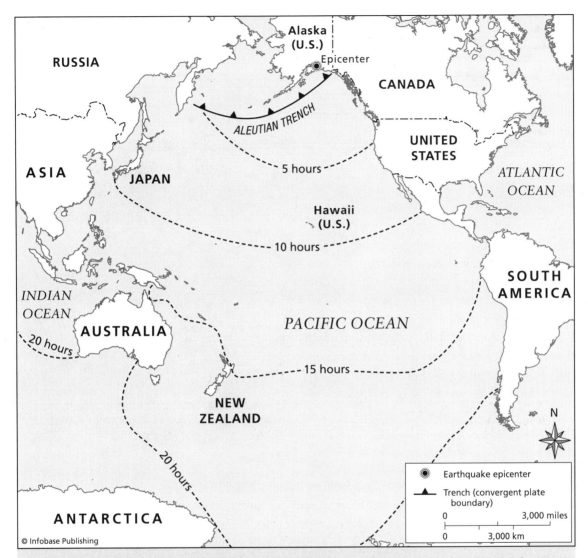

Map showing the dispersion of the tsunamis from the 1964 magnitude 9.2 earthquake. Circle shows location of epicenter and wave fronts are shown as lines stretching across the Pacific Ocean for each hour.

seichelike waves that removed much of the waterfront docks, train yards, and streets. During the earthquake, a large section of the waterfront at Seward, several hundred feet (100 m) wide and more than half a mile long (1 km), slid into the ocean along a curved fault surface. The movement of such significant quantities of material underwater generated a tsunami with a 30-foot (9-m) run-up that washed over Seward about 20 minutes after the earthquake. The earthquake and landslides tore apart many seafront oil storage facilities, and the oil caught fire and exploded, sending flames 200 feet (60 m) into the air. The oil on the waves caught fire and rolled inland on the 30–40-foot- (9–12-m-) high tsunami crests. These flaming waves crashed into a train loaded with oil, causing each of 40 successive tankers to explode one after the other as the train was torn from the tracks. The waves moved inland, carrying boats, train cars, houses, and other debris, much of it in flames. The mixture moved overland at 50–60 MPH (80–100 km/hr) and raced up the airport runway and blocked the narrow valley marking the exit from the town into the mountains. The tsunami had several large crests, with many reports of the third being the largest. Twelve people died in Seward, and the town of Seward was declared a total loss after the earthquake and ensuing tsunami and was moved to a new location a few miles away, on ground thought to be more stable from submarine landslides. Steep mountains mark the southwest side of the current town.

Aerial view of Seward after tsunami, showing destruction of waterfront and curved scalloped shoreline formed by submarine slumps removing several blocks from the shoreline *(University of Alaska Fairbanks)*

As the tsunami reached into the many bays and fjords in southern Alaska, it caused the water in many of these bays to oscillate back and forth in series of standing waves that caused widespread and repeated destruction. In Whittier, wave run-ups were reported to be up to 107 feet (32 m), and the town suffered submarine landslides that destroyed oil and train facilities. Submarine landslides, seichelike waves, 23-foot- (7-m-) high tsunami, and exploding oil tanks similarly affected Valdez. Near Valdez, the tsunami broke large trees leaving only stumps more than 100 feet (30 m) above high-tide mark. The tsunami deposited driftwood, sand, and other debris up to 170 feet (52 m) above sea level near Valdez. Like Seward, Valdez was built on a glacial outwash delta at the head of the fjord, and large sections of the delta collapsed and slid under the sea during the earthquake. A section of the town 600 feet (182 m) wide and nearly a mile (1.3 km) long slipped beneath the waters of the fjord during the earthquake, followed within minutes by a 30-foot- (9-m-) high tsunami that swept into town, killing 32 people. The natural resonance

View of destruction on the Seward waterfront *(Anchorage Museum of History and Art)*

of the bay at Valdez caused the water to oscillate for hours, so much that five to six hours after the initial tsunami, another series of waves grew and continued to wash into the town with crests moving through the town until nearly midnight on March 27. Then, another tsunami crest hit at 1:45 P.M. the following afternoon, moving through downtown as a tidal bore.

The town of Kodiak, 500 miles (800 km) from the epicenter, also experienced extensive damage, and 18 people were killed. The land at Kodiak subsided 5.6 feet (1.7 m) during the earthquake, and then the town was hit by a series of at least 10 tsunami crests up to 20 feet (6 m) high that destroyed the port and dock facilities as well as more than 200 other buildings.

Within 25 minutes of the earthquake, the huge displacements of water had organized into a deepwater tsunami that was moving southward into the open Pacific Ocean. This wave had a period of more than an hour, and in many places the first wave to hit was characterized by a slow rise of water into coastal areas, but the second wave was more powerful and associated with a steep breaking wave. When the tsunami reached the state of Washington four hours after the earthquake, it washed up in most places as a five-foot- (1.5-m-) tall wall of water and was decreased in amplitude to two feet (0.6 m) by the time it got to Astoria, Oregon. Local bays and other effects caused some variations, and the maximum waves' heights in all of Washington, Oregon, and California generally were in the range of 14–15 feet (4.3–4.5 m). However, when the wave got to Crescent City, California, the shapes of the seafloor and bay were able to focus the energy from this wave into a series of five tsunami crests. The fourth was a 21-foot- (6.3-m-) high crest that swept into downtown, washing away much of the waterfront district and killing 11 people, after they had returned to assess the damage from the earlier wave crests. This fourth wave was preceded by a large withdrawal of water from the bay, such that boats were resting on the seafloor. When the large crest of the fourth wave hit the city it washed inland through 30 city blocks, destroying waterfront piers and docks. Later analysis of the Crescent City area has shown that the bay has been hit by at least 13 significant historical tsunami and the shape of the seafloor serves to amplify waves that enter the bay.

Other locations along the California coast were luckier than Crescent City, but still suffered destruction of piers, boats, and other waterfront facilities. One potential disaster was averted in San Francisco. About 10,000 people had rushed to the waterfront to watch the tsunami as it was supposed to pass the city. These people did not know the dangers, but the shape of the seafloor and bays in this region did not amplify the waves as occurred in Crescent City, so no lives were lost. The tsunami continued to move around the Pacific, being recorded as 7.5-foot (2.3-m) waves in Hawaii and smaller crests across Japan, South America, and Antarctica.

## HILO, HAWAII, TSUNAMI, APRIL 1, 1946

On April 1, 1946, an earthquake-generated tsunami near the Unimak Islands in Alaska devastated vast regions of the Pacific Ocean. This tsunami was one of the largest and most widespread across the Pacific Ocean this century.

A lighthouse at Scotch Cap in the Aleutians was the first to feel the effect of the tsunami. At about 1:30 P.M., the crew of five at the lighthouse recorded feeling an earthquake lasting 30–40 seconds, but no serious damage occurred. A second quake was felt nearly half an hour later, also with no damage. Fifty minutes after the earthquake, the crew of a nearby ship recorded a "terrific roaring of the sea, followed by huge seas." They reported a wave (tsunami) that rose over the top of the Scotch Cap lighthouse and over the cliffs behind the station, totally

Scotch Cap lighthouse in 1929 before the tsunami and, view from above, after the tsunami of 1946  *(Anchorage Museum of History and Art; Alaska State Library)*

destroying the lighthouse and coast guard station. The lighthouse was built of steel-reinforced concrete and sat on a bluff 46 feet (14 m) above sea level. The wave is estimated to have been 90–100 feet (27–30 m) high. A rescue crew sent to Scotch Cap lighthouse five hours after the disaster reported that the station was gone and debris (including human organs) was strewn all over the place. There were no survivors.

Many hours later, the tsunami had traveled halfway across the Pacific and was encroaching on Hawaii. Residents of Hilo, Hawaii, first noticed that Hilo Bay drained and springs of water sprouted from the dry seafloor that was littered with dying fish. As the residents wondered at the cause of the water suddenly draining from their bay, a series of huge waves came crashing in from the ocean and quickly moved into the downtown district. Buildings were ripped from their foundations and thrown into adjacent structures, bridges were pushed hundreds of feet upstream from their crossings, and boats and railroad cars were tossed about like toys. After the tsunami receded, Hilo was devastated, with one-third of the city destroyed and 96 people dead. Outside Hilo, entire villages disappeared and were washed into the sea along with their residents.

## KAMAISHI (SANRIKU) TSUNAMI, JUNE 15, 1896

Twenty-seven thousand people died in a huge tsunami that swept over the seaport of Kamaishi, Japan, on June 15, 1896. A local earthquake caused mild shaking of the port city, which was not unusual in this tectonically active area. However, 20 minutes later the bay began to recede. Then, 45 minutes after the earthquake, the port city was inundated with a 90-foot- (27-m-) high wall of water that came in with a tremendous roar. The town was nearly completely obliterated, and 27,000 people, mostly women and children, perished in a few short moments. Kamaishi was a fishing port and, when the tsunami struck, the fishing fleet was at sea and did not notice the tsunami, since it had a very small amplitude in the deep ocean. When the fishing fleet returned the next morning, they sailed through many miles of debris, thousands of bodies, and reached their homes only to find a few smoldering fires among a totally devastated community.

## CHILE EARTHQUAKE AND TSUNAMI, MAY 22, 1960

The great magnitude 9.5 Chilean earthquake of May 22, 1960, generated a huge tsunami that killed more than 1,000 people near the epicenter and almost 1,000 more as the wave propagated across the Pacific Ocean. This tsunami was generated along the convergent boundary between the small Nazca oceanic plate in the Pacific Ocean and southern South America. This part of the ring of fire convergent boundary

*(opposite page)* Map of Chile showing the length of the fault segment in the trench and forearc that ruptured in the 1960 magnitude 9.5 earthquake, forming a large tsunami that swept the Pacific Ocean  *(modified from USGS)*

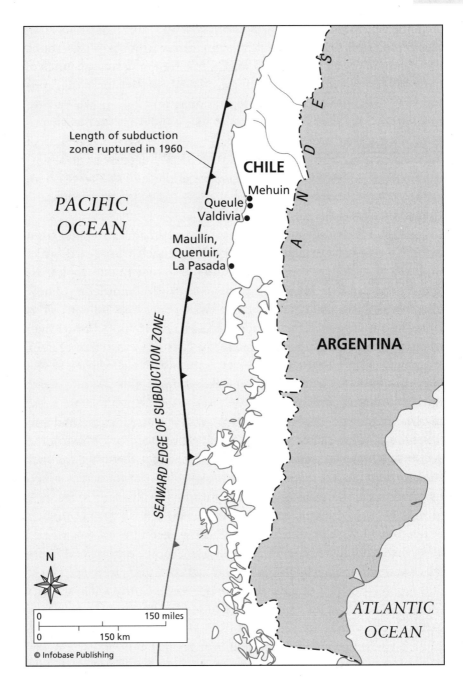

generates more tsunamogenic earthquakes than anywhere else on the planet, unleashing a large tsunami about every 30 years. Damage from the 1960 earthquake led directly to the establishment of the modern Pacific tsunami warning system.

Saturday, May 21, began as a normal day in Chile, a morning soon interrupted by a series of about 50 significant earthquakes that shook the continent beginning at 6:02 A.M. The first tremor destroyed much of the area around Concepción, with a sequence of aftershocks that continued until 3:11 P.M. the following day. Then, on May 22, two massive earthquakes exploded with magnitudes of 8.9 and 9.5, with their hypocenters located a mere 20 miles (33 km) below the surface. A section of the seafloor and coast nearly 200 miles (300 km) long experienced sudden uplift of 3.3 feet (1 m) and subsidence of the land of 5 feet (1.6 m) occurred across an area of 5,000 square miles (13,000 sq km), extending 18 miles (29 km) inland.

Since the area was (and still is) prone to tsunami generated from earthquakes, local coastal fishermen knew that such a large earthquake would likely be followed by a giant tsunami, so they rapidly took their families and ran their boats to the open ocean. This knowledge of how to respond to tsunamis undoubtedly saved many lives initially, since 10 to 15 minutes after the large quake, a large, 16-foot- (5-m-) high tsunami rolled into many shoreline areas, causing destruction of dock areas and coastal villages. However, after this wave washed back to sea, many fishermen returned or stayed close to shore. This was a mistake, since 50 minutes after the first wave retreated, another larger crest struck, this time as a 26-foot- (8-m-) tall wall of water that crashed into the shore at a remarkable speed of 125 MPH (200 km/hr). Many of the deaths in Chile were reportedly related to the fact that after the first tsunami crest passed, many Chileans assumed the danger was over and returned to the shoreline. The second crest had a run-up of 26 feet (7.9 m) and was followed by a third crest with a height of 36 feet (11 m) that moved inland at about half the speed as the second wave, but was so massive that it inflicted considerable damage. For the next several hours the coast was pounded by a series of waves that virtually destroyed most of the development along the coastline between Concepción and Isla Chiloe. Run-up heights were variable along the coast in the southern part of Chile, with most 28–82 feet (8.5–25 m). The number of people killed in Chile by this tsunami is unknown because of poor documentation, but most estimates place the number between 5,000 and 10,000 people.

The massive earthquakes of May 22 sent a series of tsunami crests racing across the Pacific Ocean at 415–460 MPH (670–740 km/hr) and around the world for the next 24 or more hours. The tsunami train had wavelengths of 300–500 miles (500–800 km) and periods of 40–80

Photo showing damage to the harbor in Ancud, Chile, 1960  *(© Bettmann/CORBIS)*

minutes between passing crests and was only a little more than a foot high (40 cm) in the open ocean. The waves swept up the coast of South America and then the western United States, where run-up heights were small, typically less than 4 feet (1.2 m). However, in some bays along the west coast of the United States run-up heights reached up to 12 feet (3.7 m). The tsunami was accurately predicted to hit Hawaii 14.8 hours after the earthquake and arrived within a minute of the predicted time. This should have saved lives, but 61 people were killed in Hawaii, including many who heard the warnings but rushed to the coast to watch the waves strike.

The response of the population of Hilo to tsunami warnings in 1960 is a lesson about the need to understand the hazards of tsunamis to save lives. As the tsunami approached Hawaii, the wave crests refracted around to the north side of the islands and hit the city of Hilo particularly hard, because of the shape of the shoreline features in Hilo Bay. Even though residents were warned of the danger, less than one-third of the population evacuated the coastal area when the warnings were issued, and about half remained after the first crest hit Hilo. Like many tsunamis, the first crests to invade Hilo were not the largest, and sightseers were surprised, and many killed, when the third crest pounded the downtown harbor and business district with a 20-foot (6-m) wall of water that carried 20-ton projectiles of pieces of the city wharf and waterfront buildings. The city suffered an inundation of five city blocks as the run-up reached 35 feet (10.7 m). Amazingly, about 15 percent of the city population stayed even through the largest waves. More than 540 homes and businesses were destroyed with tens of millions of dollars of damage ($24 million in 1960 dollars) and 61 residents of Hilo were dead.

Islands in the western Pacific were widely affected, with the height of the waves largely determined by factors such as the shape of the shoreline, slope of the seafloor, and orientation of the beach with respect to the source in Peru. Pitcairn Island was the strongest hit, with run-up heights of more than 40 feet (12.2 m) reported. The effects of wave refraction around some Pacific islands focused some of the tsunami energy on Japan, where the run-up heights exceeded 20 feet (6.4 m). The combined effects of this refraction of wave energy from the distant earthquake and natural resonance effects of some harbors that further amplified the waves made the 1960 earthquake an unexpectedly large and devastating disaster in Japan. Approximately 22 hours after the earthquake, the coast of Japan began to feel its destruction. The resonance effects caused the largest waves to grow hours after the initial wave crests hit Japan, whose east coast saw an average run-up of 9 feet (2.7 m). The resonance effects and seiching in the harbors caused the greatest damage, with 5,000 homes destroyed in Hokkaido and Honshu, and 191 people killed and another 854 injured and 50,000 left homeless. Property damage in Japan was estimated to exceed $400 million in 1960 dollars.

## Volcanic Eruption–Induced Tsunamis

Some of history's most devastating tsunamis have been generated by volcanic processes, either during eruptions, landslides from the slopes of volcanoes, or during collapse of the volcanic edifice into a caldera complex. Two of the most severe volcanic-induced tsunamis were the 1815 eruption of Tambora and the 1883 eruption of Krakatau, both in Indonesia.

### TAMBORA, INDONESIA, APRIL 5, 1815

The largest volcanic eruption ever recorded is that of the Indonesian *island arc* volcano Tambora in 1815. This eruption initially killed an estimated 92,000 people, largely from the associated tsunami. The eruption sent so much particulate matter into the atmosphere that it influenced the climate of the planet, cooling the surface and changing patterns of rainfall globally. The year after the eruption is known as the year without a summer in reference to the global cooling caused by the eruption, although people at the time did not know the reason for the cooling. In cooler climates, the year without a summer saw snow throughout the summer and crops were not able to grow. In response, great masses of U.S. farmers moved from New England to the Midwest and Central Plains, seeking a better climate for growing crops.

Tambora is located in Indonesia, a chain of thousands of islands that stretch from Southeast Asia to Australia. The tectonic origins of these islands are complex and varied, but many along the southwest part of the chain are volcanic in origin, formed above the Sumatra-Sunda trench system. This trench marks the edge of subduction of the Indian-Australia plate beneath the Philippine-Eurasian plates and formed a chain of convergent margin island arc volcanoes above the subduction zone. Tambora is one of these volcanoes, located on the island of Sumbawa, east of Java. Tambora is somewhat unique among the volcanoes of the Indonesian chain as it is located farther from the trench (210 miles [340 km]) and farther above the subduction zone (110 miles [175 km]) than other volcanoes in the chain. This is related to the fact that Tambora is located at the junction of subducting continental crust from the Australian plate and subducting oceanic crust from the Indian plate. A major fault cutting across the convergent boundary is related to this transition, and the magmas that feed Tambora seem to have risen along fractures along this fault.

Tambora has a history of volcanic eruptions extending back at least 50,000 years. The age difference between successive volcanic layers is large, and there appears to have been as much as 5,000 years between individual large eruptions. This is a large time interval for most volcanoes and may be related to Tambora's unusual tectonic setting far from the trench along a fault zone related to differences between the types of material being subducted on either side of the fault.

In 1812, Tambora started reawakening with a series of earthquakes plus small steam and ash eruptions. People of the region did not pay much attention to these warnings, not remembering the ancient eruptions of 5,000 years past. On April 5, 1815, Tambora erupted with an explosion that was heard 800 miles (1,300 km) away in Jakarta. Ash probably reached more than 15 miles (25 km) into the atmosphere, but this was only the beginning of what was to be one of history's greatest eruptions. Five days after the initial blast a series of huge explosions rocked the island, sending ash and pumice 25 miles (40 km) into the atmosphere and sending hot pyroclastic flows (nuée ardents) tumbling down the flanks of the volcano and into the sea, generating tsunamis. When the hot flows entered the cold water, steam eruptions sent additional material into the atmosphere, creating a scene of massive explosive volcanism and wreaking havoc on the surrounding land and marine ecosystems. More than 36 cubic miles (150 cubic km) were erupted during these explosions from Tambora, more than 100 times the volume of the Mount Saint Helens eruption of 1980.

Ash and other volcanic particles such as pumice from the April eruptions of Tambora coved huge areas that stretched many hundreds of miles across Indonesia. Towns located within a few tens of miles experienced strong hurricane force winds that carried rock fragments and ash, burying much in their path and causing widespread death and destruction. The ash caused a darkness like night that lasted for days even in locations 40 miles (65 km) from the eruption center, so dense was the ash. Roofs collapsed from the weight of the ash, and 15-foot-

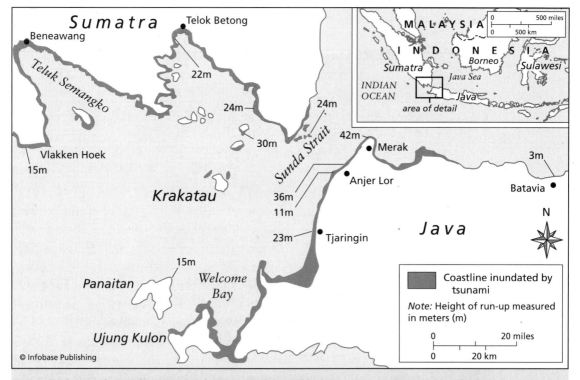

Map of Indonesia showing location of Krakatau and locations of high tsunami run-ups around Sunda Strait

(4.5-m-) tall tsunamis were formed when the pyroclastic flows entered the sea. These tsunamis swept far inland in low-lying areas, killing and sweeping away many people and livestock. A solid layer of ash, lumber, and bodies formed on the sea extending several miles west from the island of Sumbawa, and pieces of this floating mass drifted off across the Java Sea. Although it is difficult to estimate, at least 92,000 people were killed in this eruption. Crops were incinerated or poisoned and irrigation systems destroyed, resulting in additional famine and disease after the eruption ceased, killing tens of thousands of people who survived the initial eruption and forcing hundreds of thousands of others to migrate to neighboring islands.

The year of 1816 is known as the year without a summer, caused by the atmospheric cooling from the sulfur dioxide released from Tambora. Snow fell in many areas across Europe and in some places was colored yellow and red from the volcanic particles in the atmosphere. Crops failed, people suffered, social and economic unrest resulted from the poor weather, and the Napoleonic wars soon erupted. Famine swept Europe hitting France especially hard, with food and antitax riots erupting in many places. The number of deaths from the famine in Europe is estimated at another 100,000 people.

## KRAKATAU, INDONESIA, AUGUST 27, 1883

Indonesia has seen catastrophic volcanic eruptions and associated tsunamis other than just from Tambora. The island nation of Indonesia has more volcanoes than any other country in the world, with more than 130 known active volcanoes. These volcanoes have been responsible for about one-third of all the deaths attributed to volcanic eruptions and associated tsunamis in the world. Indonesia stretches for more than 3,000 miles (5,000 km) between Southeast Asia and Australia and is characterized by very fertile soils, warm climates, and one of Earth's densest populations. The main islands in Indonesia include, from northwest to southeast, Sumatra, Java, Kalimantan (formerly Borneo), Sulawesi (formerly Celebes), and the Sunda Islands. The country averages one volcanic eruption per month and, because of the dense population, Indonesia suffers from approximately one-third of the world's fatalities from volcanic eruptions and associated phenomena such as tsunamis.

One of the most spectacular and devastating eruptions of all time was that in 1883 of Krakatau, an uninhabited island in the Sunda Strait off the coast of the islands of Java and Sumatra. This eruption generated a sonic blast that was heard thousands of miles away, spewed enormous quantities of ash into the atmosphere, and initiated a huge tsunami that killed roughly 40,000 people and wiped out more than 160 towns. The main eruption lasted for three days and the huge amounts of ash ejected into the atmosphere circled the globe, remained in the atmosphere for more than three years, forming spectacular sunsets and affecting global climate. Locally, the ash covered nearby islands, killing crops, natural jungle vegetation, and wildlife, but most natural species returned within a few years.

Legends in Indonesia tell of several huge eruptions from the Sunda Strait area, and geological investigations confirm many deposits and calderas from ancient events. Recent work has revealed the presence of ancient tsunami deposits around the strait. Prior to the 1883 eruption, Krakatau consisted of several different islands including Perbuwatan in the north, Danan, and Rakata in the south. The 1883 eruption emptied a large underground magma chamber resulting in the formation of a large caldera complex. During the 1883 eruption, the islands of Perbuwatan, Danan, and half of Rakata collapsed into the caldera and sank below sea level. Since then a resurgent dome has grown out of the caldera, emerging above sea level as a new island in 1927. The new island is named Anak Krakatau (child of Krakatau), growing to repeat the cycle of cataclysmic eruptions in the Sunda Strait.

Prior to the 1883 eruption, the Sunda Strait was densely populated with many small villages built from bamboo, palm-thatched roofs, and other local materials. Krakatau is located in the middle of the strait, with many starfish-shaped arms of the strait extending into the islands of Sumatra and Java. Many villages, such as Telok Betong, lay at the ends of these progressively narrowing bays, pointed directly at Krakatau. These villages were popular places for trading ships from the Indian Ocean to stop and obtain supplies before heading through the Sunda Strait to the East Indies. In the middle of the Sundra Strait, the group of islands centered on Krakatau was a familiar landmark for these sailors.

Although not widely appreciated as such at the time, the first signs that Krakatau was not a dormant volcano, but about to become very active, appeared in 1860 and 1861 with small eruptions, then a series of earthquakes between 1877 and 1880. On May 20, 1883, Krakatau entered a violent eruption phase, witnessed by ships sailing through the Sunda Strait. The initial eruption sent a seven-mile- (11-km-) high plume above the strait and was heard 100 miles (160 km) away in Jakarta. As the eruption expanded, ash covered villages in a 40-mile (60-km) radius. For several months, the volcano continued to sporadically erupt, covering the straits and surrounding villages with ash and pumice, while the earthquakes continued.

On August 26, the style of the eruptions took a severe turn for the worse. A series of extremely explosive eruptions sent an ash column 15 miles (25 km) into the atmosphere, sending many pyroclastic flows and nuée ardents spilling down the island's slopes and into the sea. Tsunamis associated with the flows and earthquakes sent waves into the coastal areas surrounding the Sunda Strait, destroying or damaging many villages on Sumatra and Java. Ships passing through the strait were covered with ash, while others were washed ashore and shipwrecked by the many and increasingly large tsunamis.

On August 27, Krakatau put on its final show, exploding with a massive eruption that pulverized the island and sent a *Plinian* eruption column 25 miles (40 km) into the atmosphere. The blasts from the eruption were heard as far away as Australia, the Philippines, and Sri Lanka. Atmospheric pressure waves broke windows on surrounding islands and traveled around the world as many as seven times, reaching the antipode (exact area on the opposite side of the Earth from the eruption) at Bogotá, Colombia, 19 hours after the eruption. The amount of lava and debris erupted is estimated at 18–20 cubic miles (75–80 cubic km), making this one of the largest eruptions known in the past several centuries. Many sections of the volcano collapsed into the sea, forming steep-walled escarpments cutting through the volcanic core, some of which are preserved to this day. These massive landslides were related to the collapse of the caldera beneath Krakatau and contributed to the huge tsunami that ravaged the shores of the Sunda Strait, with average heights of 50 feet (15 m), but reaching up to 140 feet (43 m) where the V-shaped bays amplified wave height. Many of the small villages were swept away without a trace, boats were swept miles inland or ripped from their moorings, and thousands of residents in isolated villages in the Sunda Strait perished. Some of the frightening firsthand accounts of survivors are in the sidebar on the following page.

The tsunami was so powerful that many trees were ripped from the soil leaving only shattered stumps remaining as vestiges of the previous forest. In some places the forest was uprooted to elevations of 130 feet (40 m) above sea level. Bodies were strewn around the shores of the Sunda Strait and formed horrible scenes of death and destruction that survivors were not equipped to clean up. The population was decimated, food supplies and farmland were destroyed, and entire villages and roads were wiped off the islands or buried in deep layers of mud.

## FIRSTHAND ACCOUNTS OF THE TSUNAMI FROM THE ERUPTION OF KRAKATAU

Some of the records of events during the cataclysmic eruptions came from passengers on ships in the Sunda Strait. One of these is from a passenger on the ship *Loudon* captained by Captain Lindemann, as it was anchored off the village of Telok Betong:

"Suddenly we saw a gigantic wave of prodigious height advancing toward the seashore with considerable speed. Immediately, the crew . . . managed to set sail in face of the imminent danger; the ship had just enough time to meet with the wave from the front. The ship met the wave head-on and the *Loudon* was lifted up with a dizzying rapidity and made a formidable leap . . . The ship rode at a high angle over the crest of the wave and down the other side. The wave continued on its journey toward land, and the benumbed crew watched as the sea in a single sweeping motion consumed the town. There, where an instant before had lain the town of Telok Betong, nothing remained but the open sea."

Firsthand accounts from people on nearby islands reveal the harrowing events that they had to experience. One such account, from a Javanese farmworker who was in the fields near the village of Merak (5 miles [8 km] inland on Java) during the eruption, is related below (after Scarth, 1999):

". . . all of a sudden there came a great noise. We . . . saw a great black thing, a long way off, coming towards us. It was very high and very strong, and we soon saw that it was water. Trees and houses were washed away . . . The people began to . . . run for their lives. Not far off was some steep sloping ground. We all ran towards it and tried to climb up out of the way of the water. The wave was too quick for most of them, and many were drowned almost at my side. . . . There was a general rush to climb up in one particular place. This caused a great block, and many of them got wedged together and could not move. Then they struggled and fought, screaming and crying out all the time. Those below tried to make those above them move on again by biting their heels. A great struggle took place for a few moments, but . . . one after another, they were washed down and carried far away by the rushing waters. You can see the marks on the hillside where the fight for life took place. Some . . . dragged others down with them. They would not let go their hold, nor could those above them release themselves from this death-grip."

Survivors were in a state of shock and despair after the disaster and soon had to deal with additional loss when disease and famine took more lives. Soon, a state of anarchy took over as rural people and farmers from the mountains descended to the coastal region and engaged in ganglike tribal looting and robbery, creating a state of chaos. Within a few months, however, troops sent by the colonial Dutch government regained control and began the rebuilding of the region. Nevertheless, many of the coastal croplands had their soil horizons removed and were not arable for many decades to come. Coastal reefs that served as fishing grounds were also destroyed, so without fishing or farming resources many of the surviving residents moved inland.

Although it is uncertain how many people died in the volcanic eruption and associated tsunami, the Dutch colonial government estimated in 1883 that 36,417 people died, most of them (perhaps 90 percent) from the tsunami. Several thousand people were also killed by extremely powerful nuée ardents, or glowing clouds of hot ash, that raced across the Sunda Strait on cushions of hot air and steam. These clouds burned and suffocated all who were unfortunate enough to be in their direct paths.

Tsunamis from the eruption spread out across the Indian Ocean, causing destruction across much of the coastal regions, and around the world. Although documentation of this tsunami is not nearly as good as that from the 2004 tsunami, many reports of Krakatau document this event. Residents of coastal India reported the sea suddenly receding to unprecedented levels, stranding fish that were quickly picked up by residents, many of whom were then washed away by large waves. The waves spread into the Atlantic Ocean and were detected in France, and a seven-foot- (2-m-) high tsunami beached fishing vessels in Auckland, New Zealand.

Weeks after the eruption, huge floating piles of debris and bodies were still floating in the Sunda Strait, Java Strait, and Indian Ocean, providing grim reminders of the disaster to sailors in the area. Some areas were so densely packed with debris that sailors reported some regions appeared to look like solid ground, and people were able to walk across the surface. Fields of pumice from Krakatau reportedly washed up on the shores of Africa a year after the eruption, some even mixed with human skeletal remains. Other pumice rafts carried live plant seeds and species to distant shores, introducing exotic species across oceans that normally acted as barriers to plant migration.

On western Java, one of the most densely populated regions in the world, destruction on the Ujong Kulon Peninsula was so intense that the peninsula was designated a national park as a reminder of the power and continued potential for destruction from Krakatau. Such designations of hazardous coastal and other areas of potential destruction as national parks and monuments is good practice for decreasing the severity of future natural eruptions and processes.

Krakatau began rebuilding new cinder cones that emerged from beneath the waves in 1927 through 1929, when the new island, named Anak Krakatau (child of Krakatau), went into a rapid growth phase. Several cinder cones have now risen to heights approaching 600 feet

(183 m) above sea level. The cinder cones will undoubtedly continue to grow until Krakatau's next catastrophic caldera collapse eruption.

## Landslide-Induced Tsunamis

### THE 1958 LITUYA BAY, ALASKA, TSUNAMI

One of the largest-known landslide-induced tsunamis struck Lituya Bay of southeastern Alaska on July 9, 1958. Lituya Bay is located about 150 miles (240 km) southeast of Juneau and is a steep-sided, seven-mile- (11-km-) long glacially carved fjord with T-shaped arms at the head of the bay where the Lituya and Crillon glaciers flow down to the sea. The glaciers are rapidly retreating, and a rock spit known as La Chaussee Spit blocks the entrance to the bay and the large Cenotaph Island rests in the center of the fjord. Forest covered mountains rise 6,000 feet (1,828 m) out of the water. As the fiord is a glacially carved valley, it has a rounded floor under the sea, with a depth of only 720 feet (220 m). The rocks surrounding the bay are part of the Pacific plate, and the Fairweather fault, the boundary between the Pacific and North American Plates, lies just inboard of the bay.

At 10:15 P.M. on July 9, 1958, a magnitude 7.9–8.3 earthquake struck the region along the Fairweather fault 13 miles (20.8 km) southeast of the bay. The ground surface was displaced by up to 3.5 feet (1.1 m) vertically and 20 feet (6.3 m) horizontally in Crillon and Lituya bays. In some locations, ground accelerations in a horizontal direction exceeded two times the force of gravity and approached the force of gravity in the vertical direction. The earthquake sent a huge mass of rock plunging into the water below, released from about 3,000 feet (914 m) up the cliffs near the head of the bay next to Lituya glacier. This material landed in the water at the head of Lituya Bay and created a huge semicircular crater 800 feet (244 m) across circling the rockfall. The force of the impact of the rockfall was so great that it tore off the outer 1,300 feet (396 m) of Lituya glacier and threw it high into the air (an observer at sea reported seeing the glacier rise above the surrounding ridges). The wave generated by this massive collapse was enormous. The first wave (really a splash) soared up to 1,720 feet (524 m) on the opposite side of the bay, removing trees and soil with the force of the wave and the backwash. This splash reached heights that were three times deeper than the water in the bay. It washed over Cenotaph Island in the middle of the bay, destroying a government research station and killing two geologists stationed there who happened to be investigating the possibilities of tsunami hazards in the bay. A 100–170 foot- (30–51-m-) high tsunami was generated that moved at 96–130 MPH (155–210 km/hr) out toward the mouth of the bay, erasing shoreline features along its path and shooting a fishing trawler out of the bay into open water.

The size of the tsunami produced by this landslide was exceptional, being eight times taller than the next known landslide- or rockfall-induced tsunami, from a Norwegian fjord. Most landslides that fall into the water do not produce large tsunamis because only about 4 percent of the energy from the rockfall is transferred to the water to form waves in these events. Therefore, some geologists have suggested that the Lituya Bay tsunami may have had help from an additional source, such as a huge surge of water from an ice-dammed lake on Lituya glacier that may have been suddenly released during the earthquake, and the rockfall may have landed on this huge surge of water. However, even if this speculative release of water occurred, it still would not be enough to create such a large wave. A better understanding of this wave generation phenomena is needed and awaits further study.

Lituya Bay and others like it have experienced numerous tsunamis as shown by distinctive scour marks and debris deposits left behind. Studies have shown that tsunamis in the bay in 1853 and 1936 produced run-up heights of 400 and 500 feet (122 and 152 m) above sea level. This phenomenon was also well known to the native Tlingit, who had legends of spirits who lived in the bay who would send huge waves out to punish those who angered them.

## GIANT LANDSLIDE-INDUCED TSUNAMI IN HAWAII AND THE CANARY ISLANDS

Many volcanic islands, such as those of the Hawaiian chain in the Pacific, Reunion in the Indian Ocean, and the Canary Islands and Tristan da Cunha in the Atlantic, are built through a combination of volcanic flows adding material to a small area in the center of the island and frequent submarine landslides causing the islands to collapse, spreading the rocks from these flows across a wide area. Undersea mapping of the Hawaiian chain using sonar systems that can produce detailed views of the seafloor has shown that the island chain is completely surrounded by a series of debris fans and aprons from undersea landslides, covering a much larger area than the islands themselves. Submarine mapping efforts have discovered more than 70 giant landslide deposits along the 1,360-mile- (2,200-km-) long segment of the island chain from Hawaii to Midway Island. The age of the islands and flows increases from Hawaii to Midway,

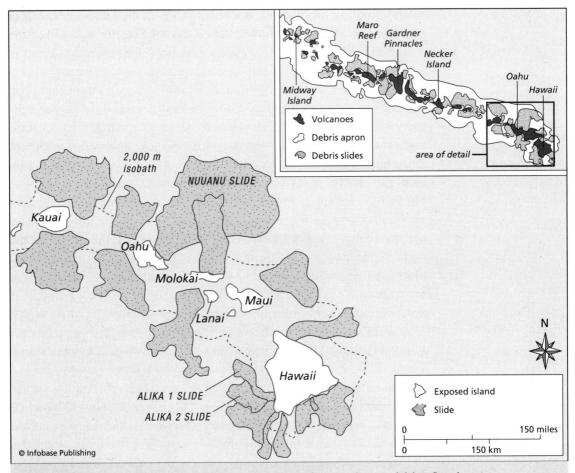

Map of the Hawaiian Islands showing the locations of the giant submarine slump and debris flow deposits

and studies have suggested that the average recurrence time between giant submarine slides along the Hawaiian chain is 350,000 years. The youngest giant slides on Hawaii, the Alika slides, are estimated to be several hundred thousand years old, suggesting that parts of the Hawaiian chain could be close to being ready to produce another giant slide.

Many of the landslides on the Hawaiian Islands are 100–200 miles (15–300 km) long, but seem to be somewhat shorter for the older volcanoes to the west. The largest ones have displaced volumes of material up to 1,200 cubic miles (5,000 cubic km). Many started on the top of the volcano near where different *rift* zones meet at the flank of the volcano. Giant slides that start near the topographic highs of the islands carve out a semicircular amphitheater on the island, and repeated slides from different directions can carve out the island into the shape of a star.

The starlike shape of many volcanic islands is therefore the result of repeated volcanism-landslide cycles, acting together to build a high and wide volcanic edifice.

Giant landslides on volcanic islands may be initiated by many causes. Most seem to be triggered by earthquakes or by earthquakes that affect slopes of volcanoes that are inflated by magma and ready to erupt. However, in other cases the volcanoes have built up such steep and unstable slopes that relatively minor events have triggered the release of giant landslides. These events have included the stresses from storm surges, internal waves in the ocean at depth, or pronounced rainfall events.

When the slopes of the volcanoes collapse they typically produce several different types of submarine slides at the same time. The submarine slides may begin at the surface or underwater as slumps, where large volumes of material move outward and downward on curved fault surfaces, some of which extend to about 6 miles (10 km) depth. These slumps can carve out huge sections of the island, but usually move too slowly to produce tsunamis. However, this is not always the case, and the Hawaiian Islands are famous for having earthquakes generated by fast-moving slumps that in turn do produce tsunamis. For instance, in 1868 a magnitude 7.5 earthquake was generated by a slump that produced a 66-foot- (20-m-) high tsunami, killing 81 people. In 1975, a 3.5 magnitude quake occurred on Kilauea when a 37-mile- (60-km-) long section of the flank of the volcano slumped 25 feet (8 m) laterally and 12 feet downward (3.7 m), forming a 47-foot- (14.3-m-) high tsunami that killed 16 people on the shoreline. Similar slumps and earthquakes are frequent occurrences on the Hawaiian Islands, but only some produce tsunamis.

The most dangerous submarine slides are the giant and fast-moving debris avalanches. These chaotic flows can start as slumps, then break into incoherent masses of moving debris that flow downslope at hundreds of miles per hour. The large volumes and high speeds of these flows make them very potent tsunami generators. The largest-known submarine debris flow around the Hawaiian Islands is the 200,000-year-old Nuuanu debris avalanche on the northern side of Oahu. This flow deposit is 150 miles (230 km) long, covers an area of 14,300 square miles (23,000 sq km), and is more than one mile (2 km) thick at its source, making it one of the largest debris avalanches known on Earth. The sheer volume of the material in this flow, which probably moved at hundreds of miles per hour, would have sent huge tsunamis moving around the Pacific. Models suggest that this debris avalanche would have caused tsunami run-ups of more than 65 feet (20 m) along the West Coast of the United States.

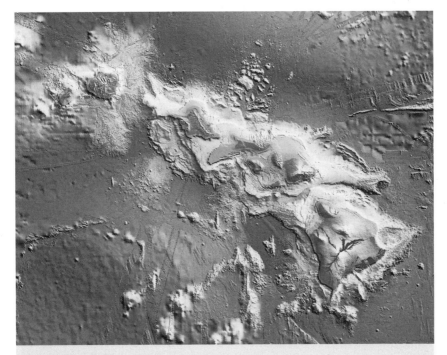

A mosaic of submarine sonar images of Hawaii *(Eakins, et al., 2003, USGS)*

Some of the younger submarine slide deposits around Hawaii that are much smaller than the Nuuanu slide have produced wave run-ups of up to 1,000 feet (305 m) on nearby islands, showing how locally devastating these slide-generated tsunamis may become. On the southwest side of the main island of Hawaii, two moderate-size slides, the 900-square-mile (2,300-square-km) Alika 1 slide and the 650-square-mile (1,700 square km) Alika 2 slide, released about 150 cubic miles (600 cubic km) of rock from Mauna Loa, excavating steep-sided amphitheaters on the island and sending the debris shooting downslope to the Pacific seafloor. Nearby islands have uncharacteristically high beach deposits that are a couple of hundred thousand years old and are probably tsunami deposits related to these slides. For instance, on the islands of Oahu, Molokai, and Maui, tsunami-related beach deposits are found at elevations of 100–260 feet (65–80 m) above sea level. On Lanai, boulder ridges form dunelike features that were deposited at more than 1,000 feet (305 m) above sea level by a catastrophic tsunami from this event. A wave with a run-up height of 1,000 feet (305 m) would need to be at least 100 feet (30 m) tall when it crashed on the coast. Areas closer to the coast on Lanai and Kahoolawe were stripped of their cover and soil to heights of 300 feet (100 m), dumping this material near the shore where it was redeposited in tsunami beds from later waves in this series of crests. This wave was so powerful when it struck the little island of Lanai that it not only removed the soil cover, but cracked the bedrock to 30 feet (10 m) depth, removing huge pieces of fractured bedrock and filling the fractures with tsunami debris.

## LANDSLIDE-INDUCED TSUNAMI OF THE CANARY ISLANDS, ATLANTIC OCEAN

The Canary Islands form a hot spot chain of small rugged volcanic islands off the northwest coast of Africa. They constitute two provinces of Spain, Santa Cruz de Tenerife and Las Palmas. The highest point on the islands is Mount Teide on Tenerife at 12,162 feet (3,709 m) above sea level, although the volcanoes actually rise more than 10,000–13,000 feet (3,000–4,000 m) from the seafloor before they rise above sea level. The Canary Islands are hot spot type shield volcanoes, very similar to Hawaii, yet they have very steep and rugged topography with amphitheater-shaped cliffs rising out of the sea, forming steep-sided mountain horns where different amphitheaters intersect. The star shape of several of the islands, together with the amphitheater shapes of many of the bays, suggests that these islands, like the Hawaiian islands, have been built by a combination of volcanic eruptions and construction of tall volcanic edifices, that have in turn collapsed

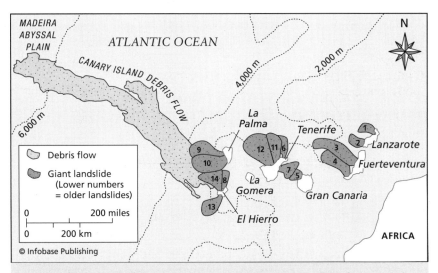

Map of the Canary Islands showing the giant landslides and debris flows that surround this intraplate hot spot volcanic island. The deposits are numbered in decreasing age, 1 being the oldest, 14 the youngest.

and spread though the action of large landslides that moves the material farther out to sea.

Mapping of the seafloor around the Canary Islands has revealed that they are surrounded by many debris avalanche deposits, giant landslide deposits, debris aprons, and far-reaching turbidites derived from the repeated collapse of the volcanic islands. A series of seven large debris flow and turbidite deposits all less than 650,000 years old are located on the west sides of the islands, some of these include 35,000 cubic feet (1,000 cubic m) of material that suddenly collapsed from the islands and was deposited at sea. On the Canary Islands, it is possible to trace landslide scars offshore into debris avalanche deposits that in turn grade into the far-traveled turbidite deposits. For instance, nearly 200 cubic miles (800 cubic km) of material derived from a five-mile- (8-km-) long, 3,000-foot- (900-m-) high headwall scarp on El Hierro Island includes huge boulders near shore, some up to three-quarters of a mile (1.2 km) across, grading in deeper water into a debris avalanche deposit that is up to 250 feet (75 m) thick. This debris flow covers about 580 square miles (1,500 sq km) and then grades oceanward into a turbidite flow that extends 370 miles (600 km) to the northwest. This deposit is estimated to be 13,000 to 17,000 years old and undoubtedly initiated a tsunami. Tsunami deposits have been identified on some of the Canary Islands, most lying at heights up to 300 feet (90 m) above sea level and one that is 650 feet (200 m) high, but so far specific slides have not been correlated with specific tsunamis. Older deposits, such as a 133,000-year-old-slide also from El Hierro, is thought to have generated a tsunami that devastated the Bahamas during the last interglacial period.

## TSUNAMI FROM SUBMARINE SLIDES ON CONTINENTAL MARGINS OF THE GRAND BANKS OF NEWFOUNDLAND AND STOREGGA, NORWAY

Submarine landslides on continental margins with steep slopes are known to have produced a number of destructive tsunamis. The cause of these slides is not always clear. Some seem to have been produced by small earthquakes, others by storms, some by rapid loading of thick and weak sedimentary layers by new sediments, and some may have been caused by the buildup and release of gas in the sedimentary sections. Several slides on passive continental margins and slopes have occurred soon after sea levels rose with the retreat of the glaciers, suggesting that the increased load of the additional water on oversteepened margins may play a role in slope failure and tsunami generation.

## GRAND BANKS SLIDE

A magnitude 7.2 earthquake on November 18, 1929, initiated a large submarine slide from the southern edge of the Grand Banks of Newfoundland. The earthquake's epicenter was located 170 miles (280 km) south of Newfoundland, and the rupture occurred 12 miles (20 km) beneath the surface. The slide involved about 50 cubic miles (200 cubic km) of material that slumped eastward, then mixed with more water and transformed into a giant turbidity current that traveled 600 miles (1,000 km) eastward at speeds of 35–60 MPH (60–100 km/hr), as determined by the times at which a series of 12 submarine telegraph cables were snapped.

The submarine slide associated with the 1929 earthquake generated the most catastrophic tsunami known in Canadian history. It had run-up heights of 40 feet (13 m) along the south coast of Newfoundland, where the waves killed 27 people. The waves penetrated about half a mile (1 km) inland and caused a total of about $400,000 (1929 dollars), including the damage to the submarine cables. The waves propagated down the East Coast of North America, killing one person in Nova Scotia and were observed at Charleston, South Carolina, and in Bermuda. The waves also crossed the Atlantic and were recorded in the Azores and along the coast of Portugal.

The Grand Banks tsunami is a very important event for understanding the present-day hazards of tsunamis along the Atlantic seaboard and in the Gulf of Mexico. The failure of the slope from an earthquake in a plate interior shows that significant risks exist anywhere there may be oversteepened thick piles of loosely consolidated sediments. Residents of coastal areas need to understand the threat from tsunamis and build structures accordingly.

## STOREGGA, NORWAY, SLIDE

The eastern coast of Norway has been the site of several large submarine landslides that have sent tsunamis raging across the Norwegian and North Seas and into the open Atlantic. The largest of these is the Storegga slide, where masses of sediment slid from the shelf to deepwater at rates of 160 feet per second (50 m/sec), or 109 MPH (175 km/hr), depositing 250–1,500-foot- (80–450-m-) thick slide deposits at the base of the slope and forming turbidite layers up to 65 feet (20 m) thick that traveled 300 miles (500 km) into the Norwegian Sea. The first well-documented slide occurred about 30,000 years ago, when about 930 cubic miles (3,880 cubic km) of sediment suddenly slipped down the steep continental slope. At this time, sea levels were low because much of the world's ocean water was being used to make the continental glaciers that covered much of North America, Europe, and Asia. Therefore, the tsunami resulting from this slide did not affect the present-day coastline. However, two younger slides at Storegga, occurring between 8,000 and 6,000 years ago, struck during higher sea levels and left a strong imprint on the modern coastline. The latter two slides were much smaller than the first, involving a total of 400 cubic miles (1,700 cubic km) of sediment. The second slide has been dated to have happened 7,950 (+/- 190) years ago and had a height in the open ocean at its source of 25–40 feet (8–12 m). The waves crashed into Iceland, Greenland, and Scotland within a couple of hours. Greenland and Iceland saw the maximum run-up heights of 30–50 feet (10–15 m), and the waves refracted into the North Sea, causing variable run-ups of 10–65 feet (3–20 m) on the north coast of Scotland. The wide range in run-up heights is due to the variable topography of the coast of Scotland and some uncertainty in the models to calculate run-up heights. These tsunamis scoured the coastline of Scotland and deposited tsunami sands and gravels 30–60 feet (10–20 m) above sea level in many places.

## Conclusion

Recent mapping of giant submarine landslide deposits around many volcanic islands in the oceans, coupled with a new recognition of the significance of large amphitheater-shaped erosional scars on many of these islands, suggests that landslides may have removed 10–50 percent of the surface of many volcanic islands. These landslides serve to spread out the steep volcanic piles that are constructed by volcanic processes, so that the volcanism and landslides together build a wide and stable volcanic island complex. Unfortunately, the submarine landslides are also capable of producing large tsunamis. Historical tsunamis in the Atlantic, Indian, and Pacific Oceans have now been related to collapse of volcanic islands, showing that even oceans that do not have subduction zones can have significant tsunami hazards. Similar submarine landslides have occurred on some *passive margins*, generating tsunamis, when thick, oversteepened sedimentary piles have become unstable from excess gas pressure, increased weight of water from rising sea levels, and pressure surges from storms and small earthquakes.

# 5

# The Indian Ocean Tsunami of December 26, 2004

One of the deadliest natural disasters in history unfolded on December 26, 2004, when a great undersea earthquake with a magnitude of 9.0 triggered a tsunami that devastated many coastal areas of the Indian Ocean, killing an estimated 283,000 people. This chapter first examines the tectonic setting of the earthquake that caused the tsunami and the seafloor rupture process that caused the ocean floor to be uplifted and displace huge amounts of water forming the tsunami. The tsunami's movement path across the Indian Ocean and its effects on coastal communities are examined and the environmental impacts of the tsunami are discussed.

The Sumatra-Andaman earthquake had an epicenter located 100 miles (160 km) off the west coast of Sumatra and struck at 7:58 A.M. local time. This was a very unusual earthquake, in that the rupture (and quake) took between eight and ten minutes, one of the longest times ever recorded for an earthquake. The hypocenter, or point of first energy release, was located 19 miles (30 km) below sea level and the rupture length of the fault extended to a remarkable 750 mile (1,200 km) length along the coast of Sumatra. Shaking from the earthquake was felt as far away as India, Thailand, Singapore, and the Maldives. The energy released by this earthquake was so great that it set the whole planet into a set of slow oscillations where all locations on the planet were vibrating back and forth by 8–12 inches (20–30 cm) initially, with a force roughly equivalent to the attraction between the Earth and Moon. The surface waves from the earthquake also traveled around the planet, producing a vibration of at least one-third of an inch (1 cm) everywhere on the planet. These vibrations gradually diminished in intensity over a period of a week, until they became so small that they were difficult to measure. The amount of energy released by this earthquake alone was roughly one-eighth of the energy released by all earthquakes on the planet in the past 100 years.

## Tectonic Setting and Earthquake

The tectonic setting of the Sumatra-Andaman earthquake was in the forearc of the active convergent margin between the Indian-Australian plate and the Burma plate of Eurasia. Oceanic crust of the Indian-Australian plate is being subducted beneath Sumatra and Indonesia at about two inches (6 cm) per year, forming a complex of volcanoes and active fault zones. The December 26, 2004, Sumatra-Andaman earthquake had characteristics that were extremely favorable for producing a large tsunami. A huge section of the forearc, 750 miles (1,200 km) long, was pushed upward and sideways by 50 feet (15 m), displacing a vast amount of water and sending it across the Indian Ocean as a giant tsunami. This displacement took place in two stages, first a 250-mile- (400-km-) long by 60-mile- (100-km-) wide rupture formed, ripping the rocks of the seafloor at a rate of 1.7 miles per second (2.8 km/sec) or, in other words, at 6,300 MPH (10,000 km/hr). This rupture not only occurred rapidly, but represents the biggest rupture known to have ever been created by a single earthquake. After a break of less than two minutes, the rupture continued to propagate northward from the Aceh area at the slower rate of 1.3 miles per second (2.1 km/sec) for another 500 miles (800 km) toward the Andaman and Nicobar Islands. Displacements of the seafloor changed the capacity of the Indian Ocean basin to hold water, slightly raising global sea levels by about 0.03 inches (0.1 mm).

Submarine sonar surveys of the seafloor by the British Navy vessel HMS *Scott* revealed that several huge, fault-related submarine ridges collapsed during the earthquake, creating submarine landslides, some as large as seven miles (10 km) across. The amount that these contributed to the formation of the tsunami is not known, but certainly less than the huge displacement of the entire seafloor of the forearc.

The vertical component of motion of the seafloor during the earthquake is estimated to have displaced about seven cubic miles (30 cubic km) of seawater, producing a tsunami that radiated outward from the entire 750-mile- (1,200-km-) long rupture area, eventually reaching most of the world's oceans including the Pacific, Atlantic, and even the

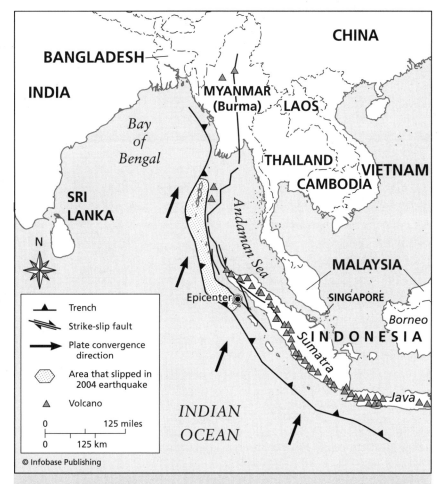

Tectonic map showing the Indian oceanic plate sinking beneath Sumatra in the Sunda trench. A line of active volcanoes on Sumatra represents the axis of the island arc system developed on the overriding plate. The magnitude 9.0 December 26, 2004, earthquake (shown by circle) occurred in the forearc of this arc, when a 750-mile- (1,000-km-) long section of the forearc was suddenly thrust upward, displacing a huge volume of water and sending it oceanward as a tsunami. *(modified from the USGS)*

Arctic Ocean. The tsunami continued to travel around the Earth for days, with very small amplitudes.

Thousands of aftershocks followed the main earthquake for days and months after the main event, gradually decreasing in strength and frequency. The largest of these was a magnitude 8.7 event that occurred on March 28, 2005, in virtually the same location along the same fault, with events of up to 6.7 continuing for more than four months after the main earthquake. A map of the distribution of aftershocks greater

Surveys of the seafloor bathymetry off the coast of Sumatra after the 2004 magnitude 9.0 earthquake, revealing giant ridges produced by displacements associated with the earthquake. These ridges are cut by amphitheater-shaped scars that were formed by submarine landslides, which probably also contributed to the formation of the tsunami. This photo taken by the remotely operated vehicle Hyper Dolphin on March 19, 2005, shows the edge of the escarpment produced by one of these landslides. *(© Japan Agency for Marine-Earth Science and Technology [JAMSTEC])*

than magnitude 4 outlines an area beneath the forearc of the Sumatra-Andaman arc that moved or slipped as a result of the earthquake. The slipped area is roughly the size of the state of California.

The amount of energy that was released in the December 26, 2004, Sumatra earthquake is staggering. Estimates vary between energy equivalents of 250–800 megatons of TNT or the amount of energy consumed within the entire United States over three to 11 days. This energy caused some interesting effects. First, the change in the shape of the Earth caused by the displacement changed the length of the day by a minute amount (2.58 microseconds). This effect is already worn off since the tidal friction of the moon increases the length of the day by about 15 microseconds per year. The change in mass distribution also changed the amount the Earth wobbles about its rotational axis by about an inch (2.5 cm), but since the natural wobble is about 50 feet (15 m), this is not a large amount and will be evened out by future earthquakes.

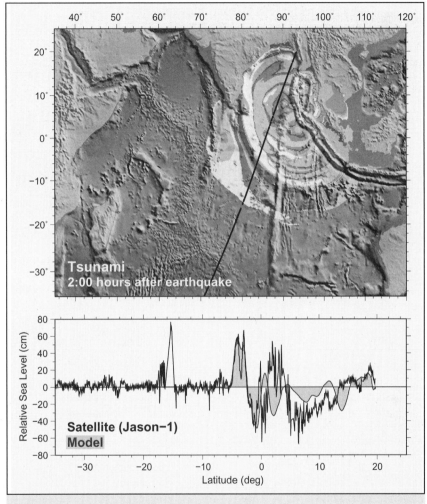

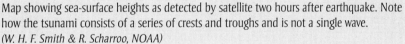

Map showing sea-surface heights as detected by satellite two hours after earthquake. Note how the tsunami consists of a series of crests and troughs and is not a single wave. (W. H. F. Smith & R. Scharroo, NOAA)

In addition to triggering one of the worst tsunami disasters of history, the December 26, 2004, Sumatra earthquake reawakened the dormant volcano of Mount Talang, which erupted in April 2005 in Aceh province. This is one of the rare cases where energy from an earthquake can convincingly be shown to have initiated other geologic activity.

The tsunami from the December 26 earthquake was unprecedented in the amount of observation that was possible from satellites. The satellite data were not analyzed until after the event and, therefore, not used to help provide a warning to areas about to be hit, but the results

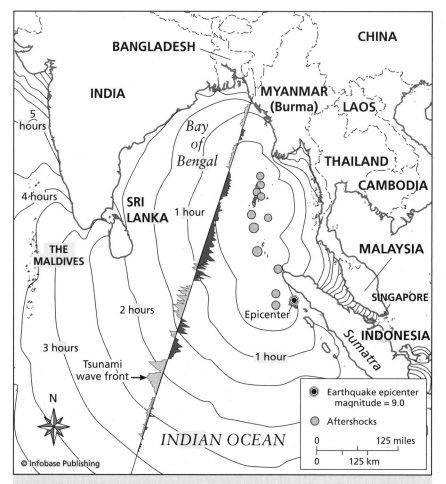

Map of the eastern Indian Ocean showing the tsunami generation area (in gray shading along the Sunda trench) and the position of the front of the tsunami at one, two, three, and four hours after the earthquake. *(modified from unpublished material of P. Shirsov, Russian Academy of Sciences)*

show that it is possible to develop a satellite-based tsunami warning system. Radar satellites showed that while in deep water, in the middle of the Indian Ocean, the tsunami had a maximum height of only 2 feet (0.6 m), the wave rose to enormous heights when it moved into shallow water. For instance, the wave was more than 80 feet (24 m) high as it approached much of Aceh province in Indonesia and rose to 100 feet (30 m) or more in some places as it moved inland. In some places the wave moved inland by more than a mile and a quarter (2 km).

The energy of the tsunami was much less than that of the earthquake, but had a remarkably high energy equivalent of about five megatons of TNT. For comparison, this is more than double the amount of energy released by all the bombs and explosions (including the atomic bombs) in all of World War II.

## Movement of the December 26 Tsunami across the Indian Ocean

Since the fault the produced the December 26 earthquake and tsunami was oriented nearly north-south and the motion of the upper plate was up and to the west, most of the tsunami's energy was focused into an east-west direction. Therefore, the biggest tsunami waves moved westward from the 750-mile- (1,200-km-) long fault rupture, while smaller waves moved out in all directions. Many areas along the coast of northern Indonesia were hit quickly, less than 15 minutes from the initial earthquake, while it took the waves 90 minutes to two hours to reach the southern end of India and Sri Lanka. The tsunami hit parts of Somalia several hours later and swept down the African coast until it struck South Africa about 16 hours after the quake with a five-foot- (1.5-m-) high crest. Tidal stations in Antarctica recorded a 3-foot- (1-m-) high wave, with oscillations lasting for a couple of days after the first wave. The energy from the wave next moved into the Pacific and Atlantic Oceans. Some unusual focusing of the wave energy may have occurred, perhaps by the mid-ocean ridge system, since some of the waves that hit the west coast of Mexico were 8.5 feet (2.6 m) high.

The Indian Ocean tsunami had tragic repercussions because there was no tsunami warning system in place in the Indian Ocean and most victims were taken by total surprise when the tsunami struck their areas. Even though the wave took hours to move around the ocean, there was not even a simple telephone communication network set up to alert residents of one coastal community that others had just perished in a tsunami, and the tsunami was moving their way. Such a simple warning system could have saved tens of thousands of lives. In a tragic twist to the story, Dr. Stuart Weinstein, a scientist from the Pacific Tsunami Warning Center, monitored the earthquake and recognized the potential for a tsunami. He frantically telephoned as many local governments as he could to warn them, but, as it was Sunday morning, most offices were closed. In cases where he

Photo of tsunami hitting beachfront at Penang, Malaysia
*(Reuters/Landov)*

Photo of flooded hotel lobby and tsunami damage in Phuket, Thailand, on December 28, 2004, two days after the tsunami struck  *(Associated Press)*

did receive an answer he was generally not believed or understood and no action resulted. Only in Madagascar did local officials listen and attempt to alert coastal residents of danger. Since the December 26, 2004, tragedy, countries of the Indian Ocean have worked with the United Nations and other countries to establish a tsunami warning system that includes not only the Indian Ocean but also the Atlantic and Caribbean.

In most places the tsunami struck as a series of waves that initially caused a retreat of the sea, followed by a large crest moving ashore. There were about 30 minutes between each wave crest that rose into coastal areas. In most places, the third wave was the largest, although many smaller tsunami crests continued to strike throughout the day. In a few locations, people recognized early warning signs of the tsunami and successfully evacuated. The most famous case is that of 10-year-old British citizen Tilly Smith, who had paid attention to her studies about tsunamis in school and knew that when the waters on the beach rapidly retreated, it is a sign of an impending tsunami. Tilly frantically warned her parents, who led an evacuation of the beach, saving many lives, as described in the following sidebar. A Scottish science teacher named John Chroston recognized similar warning signs in Kamala Bay near Phuket in Thailand and took a busload of tourists away from the beachfront, saving lives. Some native communities also recognized early

## TEN-YEAR-OLD TILLY SMITH RECOGNIZES TSUNAMI WARNING SIGNS AND SAVES 100 LIVES

A 10-year-old British schoolgirl who had paid attention in class and applied her lessons to the natural environment is credited with saving nearly 100 lives at Maikho Beach resort in Phuket, Thailand, during the December 26, 2004, Indian Ocean tsunami. Two weeks before going to Thailand on vacation with her parents, Tilly Smith learned about tsunamis in her geography class at Danes Hill School in Surrey, in a lesson taught by Andrew Kearney. Tilly was on the beach with her parents that morning and recognized the rapidly receding shoreline and frothy sea surface as warning signs of an impending tsunami. As other tourists watched in amazement, gazing at the retreating water and the violent bobbing up and down of boats in the distance, Tilly remembered her geography lesson. She became excited and told her parents of the lesson she just completed about tsunamis and convinced her parents that they were in danger and should leave the beach. In her words:

> "I was on the beach and the water started to go funny. There were bubbles and the tide went out all of a sudden. I recognized what was happening and had a feeling there was going to be a tsunami. I told my mummy."

Tilly's parents listened, alerted other vacationers to get off the beach, and told the hotel staff to help the evacuation. A few minutes after the beach was evacuated, the giant waves crashed into the beach. No one on Maikho Beach was killed or seriously injured, one of the only places in Phuket with no reported casualties.

warning signs and retreated to safety. For instance, islanders on Simeulue near the epicenter fled away from the coast after they felt the initial earthquake, undoubtedly saving many lives. In some of the more puzzling responses to precursory phenomena, it is reported that elephants and other animals on some Indian Ocean islands of the Maldives chain south of India fled inland before the tsunami struck. It is possible that these creatures, with their astute hearing, felt the ground shaking from the approaching tsunami and ran in fear into the dense forests.

## Effects of the Tsunami on Coastal Communities of the Indian Ocean

The December 26, 2004, tsunami is the worst known in recorded history in terms of the documented deaths and destruction, although the total number of deaths from the tsunami associated with the eruption of Santorini in 1650 B.C.E. and from the 1755 Lisbon earthquake are unknown. The most accurate accounting for the number of people killed by the Indian Ocean tsunami is 283,000, with another 1,690,000 people displaced. The table below breaks these casualties down by country. The number of dead contains many women and children. Many women were reportedly waiting along beaches for their husbands to return from fishing when the tsunami struck and children were not strong enough to withstand the force of the waves in coastal villages and were washed away. About one-third of the dead were children and in many locations four times as many women as men were killed. Out of the 283,000 dead, about 9,000 were foreign (mostly European) tourists. Recovery and clean-up from the tsunami was the costliest relief operation ever undertaken by the United Nations, and it may take 10 years to complete.

| Casualties from the December 26, 2004, Indian Ocean Tsunami | | | | |
|---|---|---|---|---|
| COUNTRY | DEATHS | MISSING | INJURED | DISPLACED |
| Indonesia | 167,736 | 37,063 | — | >500,000 |
| Sri Lanka | 35,322 | 6,700 | 21,411 | 516,150 |
| India | 18,045 | 5,640 | — | 647,599 |
| Thailand | 8,212 | 2,817 | 8,457 | 7,000 |
| Somalia | 289 | 211 | — | 5,000 |
| Myanmar | 500 | 500 | 45 | 3,200 |
| Maldives | 108 | 26 | — | 15,000 |
| Malaysia | 75 | 6 | 299 | — |
| Tanzania | 13 | — | — | — |
| Seychelles | 3 | — | 57 | 200 |
| Bangladesh | 2 | — | — | — |
| South Africa | 2 | — | — | — |
| Kenya | 1 | — | 2 | — |
| Madagascar | >200 | — | — | 1,000 |
| TOTAL | 230,508 | 45,752 | 125,000 | 1,690,000 |

Photo of tsunami damage in Indonesia, including boats thrown far inland  *(Reuters/Landov)*

There was much variation in the manner in which the tsunami struck in different places. In some locations, there was a drawdown of water before the first waves hit and, in others, the waves just kept appearing higher and higher. Some locations saw giant walls of water crashing into seaside resorts, while others experienced the water just rising rapidly, with strong riverlike currents carrying tons of debris through the streets. These variations were determined by the way the waves were organized near the epicenter and by local effects such as the shape of the shoreline, slope of the seabed, and how much natural and artificial protection was offshore any given location.

Photo of tsunami damage including large uprooted tree mixed with debris from homes, Nicobar, India  *(Associated Press)*

Tsunami wave crashing on Patong Beach, Thailand  (*Associated Press*)

Banda Aceh was one of the worst-hit areas since it was close to the epicenter of the quake and the tsunami hit only eight or nine minutes after the origin time for the earthquake (7:59 A.M. local time). The maximum run-up height of the tsunami of more than 98 feet (30 m) was measured at Leupung, on the west coast of Banda Aceh. Amateur video from many places in Banda Aceh show giant waves smashing into palm-lined beachfronts, washing away bathers and fishermen, and sending debris and body-laden torrents of water rushing into coastal resort villages. The run-up heights were very variable, ranging from this high to about 50 feet (15 m) along the same coast and locally only 20 feet (6 m) in other parts of Banda Aceh. Debris from the tsunami was strewn 2.5 miles (4 km) inland away from the coast. Video footage taken by tourists on the upper floors of hotels shows several wave crests, with the second or third being the highest. In some places the waves crash in a thunderous roar into the coastal communities, and in others the water just rises so fast it seems as if the sea has tipped and is spilling over into the streets of the cities.

Analysis of the damage after the tsunami shows that most houses in Banda Aceh located one–two miles (2–3 km) from shore were torn from their foundations and swept away, indicating current velocities of 25 feet (8 m) per second at one mile from shore, and 15 feet (5 m) per sec at two miles (3 km) from shore. The forward velocity was in some cases exceeded by the velocity of the retreating waters, which carried much of the debris from destroyed structures back to the sea.

## Environmental Impact of the Tsunami

The force of the tsunami on the coastal environment caused severe damage to coastal ecosystems, including coral reefs, mangrove forests, coastal dunes, wetlands, estuaries, and the groundwater system. In addition to the instantaneous destruction from the tsunami, the disaster also destroyed many systems such as sewage treatment facilities that will not be restored for years, resulting in continuing damage. Coastal erosion was severe and, in one case, exposed an ancient city buried by previous tsunami activity, as described in the sidebar below.

Many coastal reefs and mangrove forests sustained heavy mechanical damage from the force of the waves. Forests were in many places

### TSUNAMI UNCOVERS LOST CITY OF MAHABALIPURAM, INDIA

When the December 26 Indian Ocean tsunami hit the village of Poompuhar on the south coast of India, 170 people were killed and much of the town destroyed. However, the receding waves uncovered a lost city that legend says was a capital of a powerful kingdom that traded with China, Rome, Greece, Arabia, and Egypt some 1,500 years ago. It is said that the capital was "kodalkol," or "swallowed by the sea" at the height of its glory. Most archaeologists assumed that the city was gradually engulfed by rising sea levels, but the December 26 tsunami has led many to believe that the ancient city of Mahabalipuram was engulfed by a tsunami 1,500 years ago.

As the tsunami recovery proceeded, villagers noted that an ancient temple from the seventh century and a statue of an elephant had emerged from deep sands eroded from the coast by the tsunami. The ancient city of Mahabalipuram has a recorded history involving silk and pearl trading going back to the second century B.C.E. and was the capital of the Chola rulers and Tamil dynasty. The city reportedly had many foreigners who spoke all the tongues of the world and special sections were set aside for the king's soldiers. As with many prosperous Hindu kingdoms, Mahabalipuram had many temples. The one uncovered by the December 26 tsunami is thought to be just part of the main city that now lies about 2 miles (3 km) offshore. Undersea archaeological investigations have found Roman coins, brick buildings, and remnants of the ancient port.

Estimates of when ancient Poompuhar, or Mahabalipuram, was submerged vary between the third and sixth centuries C.E. Studies of the coastal sedimentary environments around southern India are likely to yield more clues about this ancient tsunami and perhaps lead geologists to understand how often events of this magnitude may be expected. Most estimates suggest that the December 26, 2004, tsunami event may be a 500-year event, meaning that events of this magnitude happen about once every 500 years.

ripped apart or totally uprooted where the force of the waves was the greatest. However, in areas where the coastal environment was least disrupted by human activity, the combined natural defenses of reefs, dunes, and forests were best able to protect coastal populations from destruction. In the Maldives, 16 of the 17 coral reef atolls that had freshwater on the inside were overwhelmed by the tsunami and are now devoid of any freshwater. These atolls could be uninhabitable for decades.

One of the most serious effects of the tsunami was the poisoning of the freshwater surface and groundwater systems and soil horizon by the salt water from the tsunami. Salt water seeped into the ground in many places through soils and fractures and porous rocks, destroying aquifers. Even after the water retreated and evaporated, it left behind a layer of salt that infiltrates the soil and the groundwater, poisoning both, making the soil sterile and killing existing plants.

## Conclusion

The December 26, 2004, Indian Ocean tsunami was one of the deadliest natural disasters in recorded history. The tsunami was generated by a magnitude 9.0 earthquake that ruptured a 750-mile- (1,000-km-) long segment of the forearc region of the Sumatra convergent margin. The earthquake displaced a segment of seafloor the size of the state of California upward and sideways about 50 feet (15 m), suddenly displacing a similar amount of water, causing the tsunami. Areas close to the epicenter, such as Banda Aceh in Indonesia, experienced a 75–100-foot- (30-m-) high wall of water rushing into beach resorts and coastal communities within minutes, killing hundreds of thousands of people. The tsunami moved across the Indian Ocean at speeds of 500 MPH (800 km/hr), hitting India, Sri Lanka, Somalia, and Madagascar with deadly waves. The tsunami then spread throughout the world's oceans, being locally amplified in places such as Mexico, but only a few inches tall in most places. The amount of energy released in the Indian Ocean tsunamogenic earthquake was enormous, greater than the energy released by all the bombs detonated in World War II. This energy caused the earth to pulsate, resonating in harmonic motions for days after the quake. The Indian Ocean was not equipped with a tsunami warning system at the time of the quake and tsunami and, if it had been, tens of thousands of lives would undoubtedly have been saved. After the tsunami, Indian Ocean nations made it a priority to establish a tsunami warning system to prepare for future events. Funds were made available by the international community, and the warning system is now in place.

# 6

# Reducing the Threat
# from Tsunamis

As more and more people move to the coastlines in the United States and worldwide, it is imperative that ways to reduce the threat from tsunamis are found. It is inevitable that tsunamis will form in the world's oceans and strike many shorelines in the years to come, but it is not necessary that these tsunamis kill a quarter-million people like the Indian Ocean tsunami of 2004 did. In this chapter, modern methods of monitoring and predicting tsunamis are discussed. The concept of mapping specific zones of high risk for tsunamis, such as places that tend to amplify the waves leading to higher run-ups, is discussed, and the need to educate the public about the signs of an impending tsunami is emphasized. The public needs to know not only how to recognize a tsunami, but what to do when one may be approaching. Different types of tsunami warning systems are discussed and methods of building along coastlines to reduce tsunami damage are examined. Finally, an assessment is made about which areas in the United States are most at risk for tsunamis in the next century.

## Monitoring Tsunami Threats

Many countries around the Pacific cooperate in monitoring the generation and movement of tsunamis. The *seismic sea wave warning system* was established and became operational after the great 1946 tsunami that devastated Hilo, Hawaii, parts of Japan, and many other coastlines around the Pacific. The seismic sea wave warning system and other tsunami warning systems generally operate by monitoring seismograms to detect potentially seismogenic earthquakes, then monitor tide gauges to determine if a tsunami has been generated. Warnings are issued if a tsunami is detected, and special attention is paid to areas that have greater potential for being inundated by the waves.

It therefore takes several different specialists to be able to warn the public of impending tsunami danger. First, seismologists are needed to monitor and quickly interpret the earthquakes and determine which ones are potentially dangerous for tsunami generation. Second, oceanographers are needed to predict the travel characteristics of the tsunami. Coastal geomorphologists must interpret the shape of coastlines and submarine topography to determine which areas may be the most prone to being hit by a tsunami, and geologists are needed to search for any possible ancient tsunami deposits to see what the history of tsunami run-up is along specific coastlines. Finally, engineers are needed to try to modify coastlines to reduce the risk from tsunamis. Features such as seawalls and breakwaters can be built and buildings can be sited in places that are outside of reasonable tsunami striking distance. Loss control engineers typically work with insurance underwriters to identify areas and buildings that are particularly prone to tsunami-related flooding. Natural defenses have been found to be very helpful at reducing tsunami run-up, as described in the following sidebar.

## REDUCTION OF LOSS FROM FUTURE TSUNAMIS THROUGH ECOSYSTEM PRESERVATION

Many countries in Southeast Asia have developing economies and often sacrifice environmental concerns to advance economic development. To this end, some of these countries including Indonesia have been promoting the development of the shipping industry and the growth of shrimp farming in coastal regions. Many coral reefs have been blown up and coastal mangrove forests destroyed to let these industries grow faster. In other places, coastal sand dunes have been removed to enhance growth of the coastal region. All of these natural ecosystems are fragile systems that not only act as habitats for a diverse set of species but also serve as a powerful shield from the force of incoming tsunamis. In areas where the reefs and forests were preserved, for instance in the Surin Islands off Thailand, the force of the tsunami was broken by these natural barriers. In other places, where these barriers had been removed, the waves crashed ashore with much greater force, killing those who would seemingly benefit by the destruction of their natural protective barrier. Many governments began to realize the value of these natural barriers after the tsunami and may make efforts to reverse, stop, or slow their destruction.

Several detailed reports have described areas that are particularly prone to repeated tsunami hazards. The U.S. Army Engineer Waterways Experiment Station has produced several of these reports useful for city planners, the Federal Insurance Administration, and state and local governments.

NOAA has been operating tsunami gauges in the deep ocean since 1986. These instruments must be placed on the deep seafloor (typically 1,500–2,000 feet [1,000 m] depth) and recovered and redeployed each year. The recordings from these instruments are sent back to shore by cables. The information derived from these tsunami gauges is used for tsunami warning systems and also for planning coastal development, since the pressure changes associated with tsunamis can be accurately recorded over long periods of time and the history of tsunami heights in given areas assessed before coastal zones are further developed.

The United States Geological Survey (USGS) runs the Pacific Tsunami Warning Center in Honolulu. It has also been actively engaged in mapping tsunami hazard areas and establishing ancient tsunami run-up heights on coastlines prone to tsunamis to help in predicting future behavior in individual areas. The results from these mapping programs are routinely presented to local government planning boards to help in protecting people in coastal areas and to assign risks to development in areas prone to tsunamis.

## Predicting Tsunamis

Great progress has been made in predicting tsunamis, both in the long term and in the short term following tsunamogenic earthquakes. Much of the long-term progress reflects recognition of the association of tsunamis with plate tectonic boundaries, particularly convergent margins. Certain areas along these convergent margins are susceptible to tsunami-generating earthquakes, either because of the types of earthquakes that characterize the region or because thick deposits of loose unconsolidated sediments characteristically slide into trenches in other areas. Progress in short-term prediction of tsunamis stems from recognition of the specific types of seismic wave signatures that are associated with tsunami-generating earthquakes. Seismologists are in many cases able to immediately recognize certain earthquakes as potentially tsunami generating and issue an immediate warning for possibly affected areas.

Tsunamis are generated mainly along convergent tectonic zones, mostly in subduction zones. The motion of the tsunami-generating faults in these areas is typically at right angles to the trench axis. After many years of study, it is now understood that there is a relationship between the direction of the motion of the fault block and the direction toward which most of the tsunami energy (expressed as wave height) is directed. Most earthquakes along subduction zones move at right angles to the trench, and the tsunamis are also preferentially directed at right angles away from the trench. This relationship causes certain areas around the Pacific to be hit by more tsunamis than others, because there is a preferential orientation of trenches around the Pacific. Most tsunamis are generated in southern Alaska (the tsunami capital of the world) and are directed toward Hawaii

Large boulders left in front of beach resort in Thailand by the 2004 tsunami  *(Associated Press)*

and glance the West Coast of the lower 48 states, whereas earthquakes in South America direct most of their energy at Hawaii and Japan.

## Tsunami Hazard Zones and Risk Mapping

The USGS and other civil defense agencies have mapped many areas that are particularly prone to tsunamis. Recent tsunamis, historical records, and deposits of ancient tsunamis identify some of these areas. Many coastal communities, especially those in Hawaii, have posted coastal areas with tsunami warning signs, showing maps of specific areas prone to tsunami inundation. Tsunami warning signals are in place and residents are told what to do and where to go if the alarms are sounded. It is important for residents and visitors to these areas to understand what to do in the event of a tsunami warning and where the escape routes may be. If there is a local earthquake, landslide, or undersea volcanic eruption, there may be only minutes before a tsunami hits, so it is essential not to waste time if the tsunami warning sirens are sounded.

## Tsunami Warning Systems

Tsunami warning systems have been developed that are capable of saving many lives by alerting residents of coastal areas that a tsunami is approaching their location. These systems are most effective for areas located more than 500 miles (750 km) or one hour away from the source region of the tsunami, but may also prove effective at saving lives in closer areas. The tsunami warning system operating in the

Photo of tsunami warning buoy being deployed off Java *(Associated Press)*

Pacific Ocean basin integrates data from several different sources and involves several different government agencies. NOAA operates the Pacific Tsunami Warning Center in Honolulu. It includes many seismic stations that record earthquakes and quickly sorts out those earthquakes that are likely to be tsunamogenic based on its characteristics. A series of tidal gauges placed around the Pacific monitors the passage of any tsunamis past their location, and if these stations detect a tsunami, warnings are quickly issued for local and regional areas likely to be affected. Analyzing all of this information takes time, however, so this Pacificwide system is most effective for areas located far from the earthquake source.

Tsunami warning systems designed for shorter-term, more local warnings are also in place in many communities, including Japan, Alaska, Hawaii, and on many other Pacific islands. These warnings are based mainly on quickly estimating the magnitude of nearby

Photo of geophysicist monitoring earthquakes at computer in the Pacific Tsunami Warning Center *(Associated Press)*

earthquakes and the ability of public authorities to rapidly issue the warning so that the population has time to respond. For local earthquakes, the time between the shock event and the tsunami hitting the shoreline may be only a few minutes. So if you are in a coastal area and feel a strong earthquake, you should take that as a natural warning that a tsunami may be imminent and leave low-lying coastal areas. This is especially important considering that approximately 99 percent of all tsunami-related fatalities have historically occurred within 150 miles (250 km) of the tsunami's origin or within 30 minutes of when the tsunami was generated.

What are the costs versus the benefits of improving tsunami warning systems for U.S. coastal areas? Which areas are most at risk? Most tsunamis that have affected the United States are generated by earthquakes in the Pacific Ocean along subduction zone convergent plate boundaries similar to the Sumatra trench that unleashed its fury on December 26. The Pacific has a warning system that can detect the deep waves and alert waiting personnel immediately of the danger. However, like the Indian Ocean, the Atlantic and Gulf of Mexico lack such warning systems. Even though the risk of tsunamis in coastal areas around these basins is much lower, the cost of a simple warning system is minor compared to the value our society places on minimizing potential loss of life. Although most tsunamis are generated by earthquakes, others are generated by landslides, volcanic eruptions, meteorite impacts, and possibly by gas releases from the deep ocean. Any of these events may happen, at any time, in any of the world's oceans.

## Knowing When a Tsunami Is Imminent

Anybody who is near the sea or in an area prone to tsunamis (as indicated by warning signs in places like Hawaii) needs to pay particular attention to some of the subtle and not so subtle warning signs meaning a tsunami may be imminent. First, there may be warning sirens in areas that are equipped with a tsunami warning system. If the sirens are sounded, do not waste time. Run to high ground immediately. People in more remote locations, such as campers on a beach in Alaska, may need to pay attention to the natural warning signs. Anyone on the shore who feels an earthquake should run for higher ground. There may only be minutes before a tsunami hits, or maybe an hour or two, or none may appear at all. However, it is better to be safe than sorry. It is important to remember that tsunamis travel in groups with periods between crests that can be an hour or more. Many people have died when they returned

Photo of tsunami warning sign in Oregon *(Associated Press)*

to the beach to investigate the damage after the first crest passes. If the tsunami-generating earthquake occurred far away, there may not be any detectable ground motion before a tsunami hits, and residents of remote areas may not have any warning of the impending tsunami, except for the thunderous crash of waves right before it hits the beachface. In other cases, the water may suddenly recede to unprecedented levels right before it quickly rises up again in the tsunami crest. In either case, anyone enjoying the beachfront needs to remain aware of the dangers. Campers in tsunami-prone areas should pick a sheltered spot where the waves might be refracted and not run up so far. In general, the heads of bays receive the highest run-ups and the sides and mouths record lower run-up heights. But this may vary considerably, depending on the submarine topography and other factors.

## Public Education and Knowing How to Respond

Communities situated in tsunami-prone areas need to educate their populace on how to respond in a tsunami emergency, especially how to follow directions of emergency officials and stay away from the waterfront. People in low-lying areas should have planned routes to quickly seek high ground, such as by climbing a hill or entering a tall building designed to withstand a tsunami. Most important, people should know NOT to return to the seafront until they are instructed by authorities that it is safe to do so, because there may be more waves coming, spaced an hour or more apart.

Many U.S. and foreign agencies have completed exhaustive studies of ways to mitigate or reduce the hazards of tsunamis. For instance, the Japanese Disaster Control Research Center has worked with the Ministry of Construction to evaluate the effects of tsunamis on their coastal road network, to plan better for inundations by the next tsunami. They considered historical records of types of damage to the road systems (washouts, flooding, blockage by debris from destroyed homes and cars, etc.) and detailed surveys of the region to devise a plan of alternate roads to use during tsunami emergencies. They have devised a mechanism of communicating the immediate danger and alternate plans to motorists. Their system includes plans for the installation of multiple wireless electronic bulletin boards at key locations, warning motorists to steer away from hazardous areas. Similar studies have been undertaken by other agencies that deal with the coastal area, such as the Fisheries Agency. They have suggested building a series of levees, emergency gates, and cutoff facilities to maintain the freshwater supply to residents.

## Tsunamis in the Twenty-First Century

Areas that have been repeatedly hit by tsunamis in the past are likely to be hit again during future earthquakes. Therefore, residents of beaches bordering the Pacific Ocean need to maintain an awareness of the potential hazards. Local officials need to plan for potential tsunami disasters, even if they only occur every 50 years. Other areas that have not seen many historical tsunamis need to be vigilant also. Some potential tsunami hazards have been identified along the U.S. East Coast. In one recent study by geologists from the Woods Hole Oceanographic Institution, Lamont-Doherty Earth Observatory, and the University of Texas, some giant submarine scarps have been identified on the continental shelf off the coast of Virginia and North Carolina. Neal Driscoll, Jeff Weissel, and John Goff believe that these scarps may represent the early stages of a large-scale submarine slope failure and that such a huge failure could generate large tsunamis that could sweep up Chesapeake Bay and along the Virginia-North Carolina coastline. What could trigger the submarine slope to suddenly fail? Earthquakes and storms are likely triggers, as are sudden releases of gases from decaying organic matter. These scientists estimate that collapse of the submarine slope off Virginia and North Carolina could easily produce a tsunami with a run-up height of greater than 10 feet (3 m). A similar slope failure off the coast of Newfoundland in 1929 formed a 30–40-foot- (10–13-m-) high tsunami, killing 28 people.

## Conclusion

It is possible to reduce the threat of tsunamis to human lives by taking a series of relatively simple steps in coastal communities. First, the risk of tsunamis from different sources needs to be assessed. In areas with a history of active faulting, submarine landslides, or volcanism, the threat from locally generated tsunami is high, whereas other areas may have high risk from tsunamis generated from distant sources. Geological mapping of the history of tsunami deposits along coastal areas can lead to a better understanding of how often a particular area is hit by tsunamis and what the run-up heights tend to be for different *recurrence intervals*. Areas of high risk should be marked with tsunami escape routes and not developed.

Tsunami warning systems have become increasingly more sophisticated. These systems are most effective for areas located several hundred miles (about 500 km) from the source of the tsunami, where there is an hour to assess the data and issue a tsunami warning. Natural warning signs of an approaching tsunami include a sudden drawdown of water levels along a beach or a low rumbling sound with huge breaking waves in the distance. A combination of public education and the establishment of tsunami warning systems is capable of saving many lives in areas that will be hit by tsunamis in the future. Areas that have the highest tsunami risk in the United States include the Pacific Northwest, where locally generated earthquake-induced tsunamis can be produced along the Cascadia subduction zone and could potentially produce large tsunamis that could strike coastal Washington, Oregon, and California within minutes after a major earthquake along this zone.

# Summary

Tsunamis are long-wavelength deepsea waves formed by the sudden displacement of large volumes of seawater. When these waves encounter shallow water, they may form huge breaking waves with walls of water tens or even 100 feet tall that slam ashore. Every few years, some of these giant waves rise unexpectedly out of the ocean and sweep over coastal communities, killing thousands of people and causing millions of dollars worth of damage. Triggering mechanisms for tsunamis include earthquake-related displacements of the seafloor, submarine slumps and landslides that displace seawater, submarine volcanism, explosive release of methane gas from deep-ocean sediments, and asteroid impacts.

Tsunamis have wavelengths of 120 miles (200 km) or greater, periods of 1.6–33 minutes, and travel at speeds of 375–600 MPH (800–900 km/hr), compared to 55 MPH (90 km/hr) for normal wind-blown ocean waves. The effective wave base for tsunamis is therefore deeper than the ocean basins, and tsunamis feel friction from the deep ocean basins and are effectively refracted and reflected around the world's oceans. When tsunamis encounter shallow water they slow their forward velocity, and the waves behind the waves in the front move faster, pile up behind the first waves, and increase the amplitude of the waves crashing onto the beach. Run-up is the height of the tsunami above sea level at the farthest point it reaches on shore. This height may be considerably different from the height of the wave where it first hits the shore and is commonly twice that of the height of the wave at the shore.

tsunamis crash into coastal areas they are commonly moving at 22 MPH (35 km/hr). The force associated with the tsunami hitting the shoreline is tremendous, as it consists at this point of a debris-laden wall of water, 50–70 miles (80–120 km) wide, moving steadily inland like an unstoppable derailed locomotive. Since tsunami are long-wavelength waves, they continue to move inland and remain high for 30–50 minutes, before rapidly retreating with a force that may exceed the force of initial incursion. Tsunamis travel in wave trains, so this processes may repeat itself six or seven times over the course of many hours, with the second or third wave often being the tallest.

One of the deadliest natural disasters in history unfolded on December 26, 2004, when a great undersea earthquake with a magnitude between 9.0–9.3 triggered a tsunami that devastated many coastal areas of the Indian Ocean, killing an estimated 283,000 people. The tsunami devastated large parts of coastal Indonesia and Thailand, then swept across islands in the Indian Ocean to strike Sri Lanka, India, and east Africa. The tsunami affected all of the world's oceans where it was locally amplified by local coastal effects, but generally did little damage outside the Indian Ocean. The Indian Ocean was not equipped with any tsunami warning system so the wave successively surprised coastal residents and tourists visiting many beach resorts. If there had been even a simple warning system in place, tens of thousands of lives may have been saved. Nations of the Indian Ocean have since invested in a tsunami warning system to prepare for future disasters.

Examination of historical tsunami events reveals that most are caused by large undersea earthquakes, since they displace vast amounts of water and can form waves that travel great distances before they dissipate. Undersea volcanic eruptions or collapse of calderas along the coast have also formed historical deadly tsunamis, with the most famous examples being the eruptions of Krakatau and Tambora in Indonesia. Volcanic eruption–induced tsunamis can be large, but since they displace less water than earthquake-induced tsunami, the waves dissipate faster than those from earthquakes. Giant landslides around volcanic islands and along continental margins have also generated large tsunamis in the historical and geological records.

It is possible to reduce the threat to coastal communities from tsunamis. First the historical record of tsunamis in any area should be determined through geological mapping and areas at greatest risk need to be identified. Residents and visitors to these areas should know escape routes and what to do in the event of a tsunami emergency. Most ocean basins now have seismic sea wave warning systems installed, where scientists monitor triggering mechanism such as earthquakes and sea-bottom pressure and motion detectors that tell of passing tsunamis. Warnings can be issued to coastal communities when it is determined that a tsunami may be approaching. Public education programs should teach the public about the hazards of tsunamis, since many of the deaths from tsunamis have been preventable. For instance, many people have perished because they have returned to coastal areas after the first wave crest has passed, not realizing that the second or third crest may be the largest and may hit hours after the first wave crashes ashore. Areas in the United States most at risk include the Pacific Northwest, where a potentially tsunamogenic forearc zone is located close to densely populated coastal areas. Any large earthquake in this area could form a tsunami that crashes in coastal communities within minutes of the earthquake, barely giving residents enough time to evacuate to higher ground. Most other coastal areas of the United States also have some risk of tsunami, so all coastal residents need to be aware of the risks and how to respond in a tsunami emergency.

# Glossary

**abyssal plains**—Stable, flat parts of the deep ocean floor are called abyssal plains. They are typically covered with fine-grained sedimentary deposits called deep-sea oozes, derived from the small skeletons of siliceous organisms that fell to the seafloor.

**amplification**—A process of transferring energy along the wave crest, as they are forced to become shorter lengthwise, causing the wave height to increase.

**amplitude**—One-half of the wave height in a wave train, measured from the bottom of the trough to the top of the crest.

**asthenosphere**—Weak partially molten layer in the Earth beneath the lithosphere, extending to about 155 miles (250 km) depth. The lithosphere slides on this weak layer, enabling plate tectonics to operate.

**barrier island**—A long broad sandy island that lies parallel to a shore and had been built up by the waves and the wind. It protects the shore from the ocean.

**basalt**—The most common igneous rock of the oceanic crust. Its subvolcanic or plutonic equivalent is called gabbro and its mineralogy includes plagioclase, clinopyroxene, and olivine.

**bore**—A wave that forms in some bays and estuaries, where the shape of the coastline tends to funnel water from the rising tides into narrower and narrower places, causing the water to pile up. When this happens, the volume of water entering the bay forms a wave called a tidal bore that moves inland, typically growing in height and forward velocity as the bay becomes narrower and narrower.

**caldera**—A roughly circular or elliptical depression, often occupied by a lake, that forms when the rocks above a subterranean magma mass collapse into the magma during a cataclysmic eruption.

**continental shelf**—Fairly flat areas on the edges of the continents, underlain by continental crust with shallow water. Sedimentary deposits on continental shelves include muds, sands, and carbonates.

**convergent boundaries**—Places where two plates move toward each other, resulting in one plate sliding beneath the other when a dense oceanic plate is involved, or collision and deformation when continental plates are involved. These types of plate boundaries may have the largest of all earthquakes.

**Coriolis effect**—This effect, or force, produces a deflection of moving objects and currents to the right in the Northern Hemisphere and to the left in the Southern Hemisphere.

**diffraction**—A process that occurs when energy moves or is leaked sideways along a wave crest, enabling the wave to grow along the wave front to fill the available area inside a wide bay that the wave has entered through a narrow opening.

**dike**—Any tablular, parallel-sided igneous intrusion that generally cuts across layering in the surrounding rocks.

**dispersion**—A process that moves energy from the initially high wave crest sideways and, in doing so, takes energy away from the central area, decreasing the height of the wave.

**divergent boundaries**—Divergent boundaries or margins are where two plates move apart, creating a void that is typically filled by new oceanic crust that wells up to fill the progressively opening hole.

**drawdown**—The rapid retreat of water from a coastline immediately before a tsunami hits. The drawdown may resemble a rapidly retreating tide.

**earthquake**—A sudden release of energy from slip on a fault, an explosion, or other event that causes the ground to shake and vibrate, associated with passage of waves of energy released at its source. An earthquake originates in one place and then spreads out in all directions along the fault plane.

**edge waves**—A secondary wave associated with tsunamis and other waves that forms as the water from one wave crest retreats and moves back to sea and interacts with the next incoming wave. Some of this water moves quickly sideways along the coast, setting up a new independent set of waves that oscillates up and down in amplitude along the coast, typically with a wavelength that is double that of the original tsunami.

**fetch**—The distance over which the wind blows over water, forming waves of a particular wave set.

**focus**—The point in the Earth where the earthquake energy is first released and represents the area on one side of a fault that actually moves relative to the rocks on the other side of the fault plane. After the first slip event the area surrounding the focus experiences many smaller earthquakes as the surrounding rocks also slip past each other to even out the deformation caused by the initial earthquake shock.

**forearc**—The part of a convergent margin between the active magmatic arc and the trench. Many tsunami are generated by thrust-type earthquakes that uplift large sections of the forearc, displacing huge masses of water.

**gas hydrates**—Decaying organic matter on the seafloor releases large volumes of gas, such as methane. Under some circumstances, including cold water at deep depths, these gases may coagulate forming gels called gas hydrates. Gas hydrates, or clathrates, are solid, ice-like water-gas mixtures that form at temperatures between 40–43°F (4–6°C) and pressures above 50 atmospheres. Large parts of the ocean floor are covered by deposits of gas hydrates. They form on deep marine continental margins and in polar continental regions, often below the seafloor. These solid icelike substances are made of cases of ice molecules enclosing gas molecules that are typically methane, but may include ethane, butane, propane, carbon dioxide, and hydrogen sulfides.

**ground motion**—Shaking and other motion of the ground associated with the passage of seismic waves. The amount of ground motion associated with an earthquake generally increases with the magnitude of the earthquake, but depends also on the nature of the substratum. Ground motions are measured as accelerations, which is the rate of change of motion.

**hot spot**—An area of unusually active magmatic activity that is not associated with a plate boundary. Hot spots are thought to form above a plume of magma rising from deep in the mantle.

**island arc**—See **magmatic arc.**

**lahar**—A mudflow formed by the mixture of volcanic ash and water. Lahars are common on volcanoes, both during and for years after major eruptions.

**lava**—Magma, or molten rock, that flows at the surface of the Earth

**lithosphere**—Rigid outer shell of the Earth that is about 75 miles (125 km) thick under continents and 45 miles (75 km) thick under oceans. The basic theorem of plate tectonics is that the lithosphere of the Earth is broken into about 12 large rigid blocks or plates that are all moving relative to one another.

**magma**—Molten rock, at high temperature, is called magma. When magma flows on the surface it is known as lava.

**magmatic arc**—A line of volcanoes and igneous intrusions that forms above a subducting oceanic plate along a convergent margin. Island arcs are built on oceanic crust and continental margin magmatic arcs are built on continental crust.

**mass wasting**—The movement of material downhill without the direct involvement of water.

**mid-ocean ridge system**—A 40,000-mile- (65,000-km-) long mountain ridge that runs through all the major oceans on the planet. The mid-ocean ridge system includes vast outpourings of young lava on the ocean floor and represents places where new oceanic crust is being generated by plate tectonics.

**morphodynamics**—The study of the effects of local coastal features on tsunami characteristics.

**nuée ardent**—A fast-moving glowing hot cloud of ash that can move down the flanks of volcanoes at hundreds of miles per hour during eruptions. Nuée ardents have been responsible for tens of thousands of deaths during volcanic eruptions.

**passive margin**—A boundary between continental and oceanic crust that is not a plate boundary, characterized by thick deposits of sedimentary rocks. These margins typically have a flat shallow water shelf, then a steep drop-off to deep ocean floor.

**plate tectonics**—A model that describes the process related to the slow motions of more than a dozen rigid plates of solid rock around the surface of the Earth. The plates ride on a deeper layer of partially molten material that is found at depths starting at 60–200 miles (100–320 km) beneath the surface of the continents and 1–100 miles (1–160 km) beneath the oceans.

**Plinian**—A type of volcanic eruption characterized by a large, tall eruption column, typically reaching tens of thousands of feet into the air. Named after Pliny the Elder, from his eyewitness description of Vesuvius

**pyroclastic**—A general term for rocks and material that are thrown from a volcano, including the explosive ash, bombs, and parts of the volcano ripped off the slopes during eruptions

**recurrence interval**—The average repeat time for earthquakes along a specific segment of a fault, based on the statistics of how frequently earthquakes of specific magnitude occur along individual segments of faults

**refraction**—The process of bending a wave front around an object, typically caused by friction on the base of the wave slowing its progress as it encounters shallow water, while parts of the wave still in deeper water continue to move quickly

**resonate**—A process of oscillating back and forth. Many bodies have a specific rate or frequency at which they naturally resonate when excited with energy, known as a natural resonance. If a wave such as a tsunami excites the natural resonance of a harbor, then the height of a wave can be dramatically increased.

**rifts**—Long topographic depressions, typically with faults along their margins, where the entire thickness of the lithosphere has ruptured in extension. These are places where the continents are beginning to break apart and, if successful, may form new ocean basins.

**rogue waves**—Unlike normal waves that lose energy and decrease in amplitude as they interact with other waves and move away from where they are generated, these waves interact with currents in a way that dramatically increases their amplitude, forming huge towering crests. Some of these rogue waves have been reported to be hundreds of feet high.

**run-up**—The height of the tsunami above sea level at the farthest point it reaches on the shore.

**seafloor spreading**—The process of producing new oceanic crust, as volcanic basalt pours out of the depths of the Earth, filling the gaps generated by diverging plates. Beneath the mid-ocean ridges, magma rises from depth in the mantle and forms chambers filled with magma just below the crest of the ridges. The magma in these chambers erupts out through cracks in the roof of the chambers and forms extensive lava flows on the surface. As the two different plates on either side of the magma chamber move apart, these lava flows continuously fill in the gap between the diverging plates, creating new oceanic crust.

**seiche wave**—An oscillation on the surface of a landlocked body of water such as a lake.

**seismic sea wave warning system**—A tsunami warning system in the Pacific Ocean that operates by monitoring seismograms to detect potentially seismogenic earthquakes, then monitors tide gauges to determine if a tsunami has been generated.

**slump**—A type of mass wasting where a large mass of rock or sediment moves downward and outward along an upward curving fault surface. Slumps may occur undersea or on the land surface.

**solar nebula**—The cloud of gases and solids in the early solar system from which the sun and planets condensed and accreted.

**storm surge**—Storm surges consist of water that is pushed ahead of storms and typically moves on land as exceptionally high tides in front of severe ocean storms such as hurricanes.

**strike-slip fault**—A vertical or nearly vertical fault that has horizontal or nearly horizontal motion along the fault

**subduction**—The destruction of oceanic crust and lithosphere by sinking back into the mantle at the deep ocean trenches. As the oceanic slabs go down, they experience higher temperatures that cause rock melts or magmas to be generated, which then move upward to intrude the overlying plate. Since subduction zones are long narrow zones where large plates are being subducted into the mantle, the melting produces a long line of volcanoes above the downgoing plate and forms a volcanic arc. Depending on what the overriding plate is made of, this arc may be built on either a continental or on an oceanic plate

**subsidence**—Sinking of one surface, such as the land, relative to another surface, such as sea level

**teleseismic**—Earthquake waves that travel from great distances and arrive from vertically below the observer are said to be teleseismic events. These are generally from large earthquakes on the opposite side of the Earth and travel through the deep interior of the Earth.

**thrust**—A contractional fault, or a reverse fault, generally with shallow dips

**tidal range**—The range in sea surface height between high and low tide.

**transform boundaries**—Places where two plates slide past each other, such as along the San Andreas Fault in California, often with large earthquakes.

**tsunami**—A giant harbor or deepwater wave, with long wavelengths, initiated by submarine landslides, earthquakes, volcanic eruptions, or other causes that suddenly displace large amounts of water. Tsunamis can be much larger than normal waves when they strike the shore and cause great damage and destruction.

**tsunamogenic earthquakes**—A special category of earthquakes that generates tsunamis that are unusually large for the earthquake's magnitude.

**turbidity current**—Sudden movements of water-saturated sediments that move down submarine slopes under the force of gravity.

**volcanic arc**—A line of volcanoes that forms above a subducting oceanic plate at a convergent boundary. See also **magmatic arc.**

**wave base**—In deepwater ocean waves, the particle motion follows roughly circular paths, where particles move approximately in a circle and return back to their starting position after the wave passes. The amount of circular motion decreases gradually with depth, until a depth that equals one-half of the wavelength. At this depth, all motion associated with the passage of the wave stops, and the water beneath this point experiences no effect from the passage of the wave above. This depth is known as the wave base.

**wave fronts**—Imaginary lines drawn parallel to the wave crests; the wave moves perpendicular to the wave fronts.

**wave height**—The vertical distance from the crest to the bottom of the trough of a wave.

**wavelength**—The distance between successive troughs or crests on a wave train.

**wave period**—The time (in seconds) that it takes successive wave crests to pass a point.

**wave train**—Waves of a certain character in a series, moving across the ocean or other body of water.

**wave trap**—Some bays and other places along some shorelines amplify the effects of waves that come in from a certain direction, making run-ups higher than average. These areas are called wave traps.

# Further Reading and Web Sites

## BOOKS

Bernard, E. N., ed. *Tsunami Hazard: A Practical Guide for Tsunami Hazard Reduction.* Dordrecht, The Netherlands: Kluwer Academic Publishers, 1991. This is a technical book on methods for coastal communities to reduce the threat of tsunami damage to the local infrastructure.

Blong, Russel J. *Volcanic Hazards, A Sourcebook on the Effects of Eruptions.* New York: Academic Press, 1984. This book discusses the geological hazards associated with volcanic eruptions.

Booth, J. S., D. W. O'Leary, P. Popencoe, and W. W. Danforth. *US Atlantic continental slope landslides: Their distribution, general attributes, and implications.* Reston, Va.: United States Geological Survey Bulletin, 2002, 1993. This bulletin produces a catalog of known submarine landslides on the Atlantic seaboard and discusses the implications for future tsunami hazards.

Bryant, E. *Tsunami: The Underrated Hazard.* Cambridge, England: Cambridge University Press, 2001. This is a general book for specialists and generally advanced readers on many aspects of tsunamis, especially on the coastal landforms formed by tsunamis.

Kusky, T. M. *Geologic Hazards, A Sourcebook.* Westport, Conn.: Greenwood Press, 2002. A general book on hazards.

Okazaki, S., K. Shibata, and N. Shuto. A road management approach for tsunami disaster planning. In Tsuchiya, Y., and N. Shuto, eds. *Tsunami: Progress in Prediction Disaster Prevention and Warning.* Boston: Kluwer Academic Publishers, 1995. This book presents an analysis on how road systems in Japan can be modified to allow coastal residents to escape during a tsunami.

Simkin, T., and R. S. Fiske. *Krakatau 1883: The Volcanic Eruption and Its Effects.* Washington, D.C.: Smithsonian Institution Press, 1993. This book presents descriptions of the effects of the eruption of Krakatau.

Steinbrugge, K. V. *Earthquakes, Volcanoes, and Tsunamis, An Anatomy of Hazards.* New York: Skandia America Group, 1982. This is a technical book covering the natural hazards associated with earthquakes, volcanoes, and tsunamis.

Tsuchiya, Y., and N. Shuto, eds. *Tsunami: Progress in Prediction Disaster Prevention and Warning.* Boston: Kluwer Academic Publishers, 1995. A technical book covering aspects of tsunami warning systems, prediction, and prevention of damage.

## JOURNAL ARTICLES

Dawson, A. G., and S. Shi. "Tsunami Deposits." *Pure and Applied Geophysics* 157 (2000). This article describes the physical characteristics of sediments deposited by tsunamis.

Driscoll, N. W., J. K. Weissel, and J. A. Goff. "Potential for large-scale submarine slope failure and tsunami generation along the U.S. mid-Atlantic coast." *Geology* 28 (2000). This paper presents evidence that parts of the continental slope along the eastern coast of the United States may be on the verge of failure and could generate tsunamis along the Atlantic seaboard.

Dvorak, J., and T. Peek. "Swept away." *Earth* 2 (1993). This is a well-written description of the effects of tsunamis on coastal communities.

"Girl, 10, used geography lesson to save lives." *News Telegraphy* (January 1, 2005). This newspaper article describes the educated actions of 10-year-old Tilly Smith, who warned her parents that the retreat of water from their vacation beach meant a tsunami was imminent.

Harinarayana, T., and N. Hirata. "Destructive earthquake and disastrous tsunami in the Indian Ocean, What next?" *Gondwana Research* 8 (2005). These authors present a description of the 2004 Indian Ocean earthquake and tsunami and present the case for future tsunamogenic earthquakes and the need to establish a tsunami warning system.

Knight, W. "Asian tsunami seabed pictured with sonar." *New Scientist* (February 10, 2005). This article contains spectacular images of the disruption of the seafloor by faults and slumps related to the 2004 Sumatra earthquake.

Latter, J. H. "Tsunami of volcanic origin, Summary of causes, with particular reference to Krakatau, 1883." *Journal of Volcanology* 44 (1981). This technical paper describes volcanic-induced tsunami and presents descriptions of the effects of the 1883 tsunami from the eruption of Krakatau.

Lay, T., H. Kanamori, C. Ammon, M. Nettles, S. Ward, R. Aster, S. Beck, S. Bilek, M. Brudzinski, R. Butler, H. DeShon, G. Ekström, K. Satake, and S. Sipkin. *"The Great Sumatra-Andaman Earthquake of December 26, 2004."* Science 308 (2005). This technical paper defines the magnitude and length of rupture of the 2004 Sumatra earthquake that initiated the 2004 Indian Ocean tsunami.

McCoy, F., and G. Heiken. *"Tsunami generated by the late Bronze age eruption of Thera (Santorini), Greece."* Pure and Applied Geophysics 157 (2000). This paper presents historical and geological evidence that a giant tsunami was generated by the eruption of Santorini and devastated the Mediterranean in the late Bronze age, wiping away the Minoan civilization.

McKee, Maggie. *"Radar satellites capture tsunami wave height."* New Scientist (January 6, 2005). This paper presents a nontechnical review of the detection of the 2004 Indian Ocean tsunami by radar satellites.

Minoura, K., F. Imamura, T. Takahashi, and N. Shuto. *"Sequence of sedimentation processes caused by the 1992 Flores tsunami, Evidence from Babi Island."* Geology 25 (1997). This paper describes and reconstructs the 1992 Flores tsunami based on evidence from tsunami deposits around the island of Flores and Babi.

Minoura, K., F. Inamura, T. Nakamura, A. Papadopoulos, T. Takahashi, and A. Yalciner. "Discovery of Minoan tsunami deposits." *Geology* 28 (2000). This paper supports the idea that a giant tsunami was generated by the eruption of Santorini and destroyed the Minoan civilization in the late Bronze age.

Pearce, Fred. "Tsunami's salt water may leave islands uninhabitable." *New Scientist* (January 5, 2005). In this review, salt water moved by the 2004 Indian Ocean tsunami is described as a hazard, seeping into water supplies and agricultural lands.

Revkin, A. C. "Tidal Waves called threat to East Coast." *The New York Times* (July 14, 2000). Evidence that the Atlantic Ocean experiences tsunami is presented in this nontechnical article.

Satake, K. "Tsunamis." *Encyclopedia of Earth System Science* 4 (1992). This basic review discusses the general characteristics of tsunamis.

"Tsunami waves exposed remnants of lost city." *New Scientist* (February 26, 2005). This newspaper article described how the 2004 Indian Ocean tsunami eroded the beach in part of southern India, exposing an ancient city that was probably buried by an ancient tsunami.

USGS. "Surviving a Tsunami-Lesson from Chile, Hawaii, and Japan." Circular 1187, 1987. This information circular by the USGS gives tips on what to do and not to do during a tsunami.

Yeh, H., F. Imamura, C. Syndakis, Y. Tsuji, P. Liu, and S. Shi. "The Flores Island tsunami." *EOS, Transactions of the American Geophysical Union* 73 (1993). This article is a technical description of the causes and effects of the 1992 Flores Island tsunami.

## INTERNET RESOURCES

In the past few years numerous internet Web sites that have information about tsunamis have appeared, many focused on the 2004 Indian

Ocean tsunami. Most of these are free and include historical information about specific tsunamis, real-time monitoring of tsunami warnings around the world, and educational material. Many other sites offer movie clips and before and after photos from specific locations affected by the 2004 Indian Ocean tsunami. The sites listed below have interesting information and graphics about these tsunamis. This book may serve as a useful companion while surfing through the information on the internet when encountering unfamiliar phrases, terms, or concepts not fully explained on the Web site. The following list is recommended to help enrich the content of this book and make your exploration of tsunami hazards more enjoyable. In addition, any tsunamis that occur after this book goes to press will be discussed on these Web sites, so checking them can help you keep this book up to date. From these Web sites you will also be able to link to a large variety of tsunami and hazard-related sites. Every effort has been made to ensure the accuracy of the information provided. However, due to the dynamic nature of the internet, changes might occur and any inconvenience is regretted.

**Incorporated Research Institutions for Seismology (IRIS).** Available online. URL: http://www.iris.iris.edu/sumatra. Accessed March 28, 2007. This Web site provides many of the technical details about the nature of the earthquake that generated the tsunami. It include many downloadable graphics.

**Los Alamos National Laboratory, Tsunami Society.** Available online. URL: http://library.lanl.gov/tsunami. Accessed March 28, 2007. Site publishes an online journal in pdf format available for download, called the International Journal of the Tsunami Society. The journal comes out between two and five times per year.

**National Oceanographic and Atmospheric Administration, hazards research.** Available online. http://ngdc.noaa.gov/seg/hazard/tsu.html. Accessed March 28, 2007. Web site about hazards, including tsunami.

———, **Pacific Tsunami Warning Center.** Available online. URL: http://www.prh.noaa.gov/ptwc. This site, run by NOAA, posts information on recent tsunami threats for all the world's oceans.

———, **tsunami research program.** Available online. URL: http://www.pmel.noaa.gov/tsunami. Accessed March 28, 2007. Web site of the tsunami research program at NOAA.

**National Tsunami Hazard Mitigation Program.** Available online. URL: http://nthmp-history.pmel.noaa.gov/index.html. Accessed March 28, 2007. This is a partnership between the states of Hawaii, Alaska, California, Oregon, and Washington and FEMA, NOAA, and USGS. This program is preparing maps showing tsunami inundation areas and implementing mitigation plans for the states in the program. The NTHMP is also developing an early warning system, including seismic stations and deep ocean tsunami detectors.

**Pacific Tsunami Warning Center.** Available online. URL: https://www. mcahawaii.com/grps07/aseehi2007/tsunami.html. Established in 1949, the Pacific Tsunami Warning Center (PTWC) located in Ewa Beach, Hawaii, provides warnings for teletsunamis to most countries in the Pacific basin as well as to Hawaii and all other U.S. interests in the Pacific outside of Alaska and the U.S. West Coast. Those areas are served by the West Coast/Alaska Tsunami Warning Center (WC/ATWC) in Palmer, Alaska. PTWC is also the warning center for Hawaii's local and regional tsunamis. The center uses seismic data as its starting point, but then takes into account oceangraphic data when calculating possible threats. Tide gauges in the area of the earthquake are checked to establish if a tsunami wave has formed. The center then forecasts the future of the tsunami, issuing warnings to at-risk areas all around the Pacific basin if needed.

**St. Louis University Center for Environmental Science.** Available online. URL: http://CES.SLU.EDU. Accessed May 9, 2007. This site has discussions of many types of geologic hazards, including earthquakes, volcanoes, tsunamis, hurricanes, and how these geologic phenomena are affecting people.

**Tsunamis.com.** Available online. URL: http://www.tsunamis.com/tsunami-pictures.html. Accessed March 28, 2007. This Web site posts many photographs of effects of the December 26, 2004, Indian Ocean tsunami.

**USGS, Tsunami Research Program.** Available online. URL: http://walrus.wr.usgs.gov/tsunami. Accessed March 28, 2007. This Web site highlights ongoing research in tsunami hazards and disasters by USGS personnel.

# Index

Note: Page numbers in *italic* refer to illustrations; *m* indicates a map; *t* indicates a table.